"I never saw a man
so drunk with God."

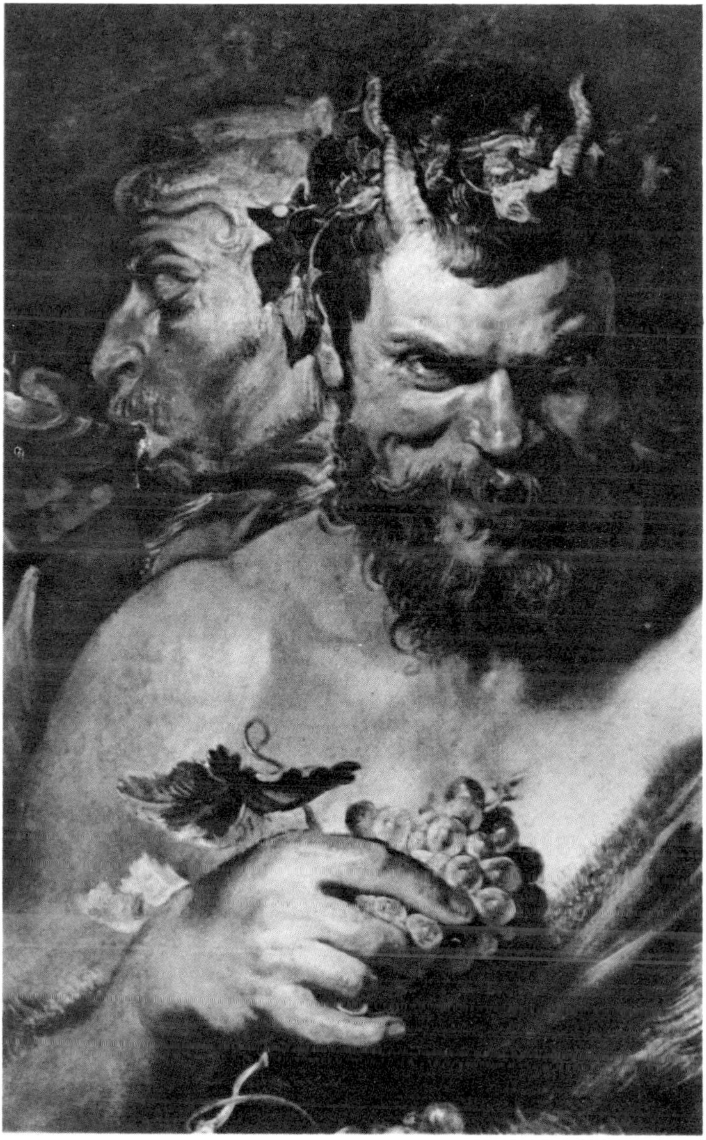

ALCOHOLISM
THE HIDDEN SIGNIFICANCE

DOUGLAS BAKER
B.A. M.R.C.S. L.R.C.P.

First Edition 1977
This Edition 1991

ISBN 0 90600 606 6

Published by:
Baker Publications,
'Little Elephant', High Road, Essendon, Hertfordshire.

Printed by:
Zodiac Books Ltd,
Unit 8, Caxton Hill Industial Estate, Hertford, Hertfordshire.

Contents

Author's Note

The stress imposed upon us by our modern way of life—its competitiveness reinforced by both church and school, its standard of living, its codes of conduct, its ethics, its laws—all contribute to a situation in which we are subjected to sustained, unremittent stress. After the Second World War, most of us fondly believed it would be merely a matter of time before the stress which was mounted by that mighty operation would be alleviated, but it wasn't. Then, we blamed the Iron Curtain, and the population increase, and the unequal distribution of wealth, etc., etc. as causes of our stress. Now we have to face up to the bitter fact that stress is here to stay. It is part of our way of life. More than this, it is a challenge presented to the fifth subrace.

Now, this stress, common to all in the west, is reaching such proportions that many are hard put to cope with it. Indeed, few, only a very few, know how to approach the problem, and of these, less even know what are the causes of the increasing stress. Not only is the factor of stress here to stay, but it is one that is essential for the spiritual unfoldment of the race. The problems of evolving spiritual techniques for dealing with this entirely unique situation have been dealt with in my other works, especially in *The Psychology of Discipleship* and *In the Steps of the Master*.

But what about the individual who has failed in his ability to cope with these mountains of stress, and has resorted to the Nirvana of the bottle to find relief—however temporary—from his daily frustrations and dissatisfaction with his life circumstances?

It is quite possible that many alcoholics have sound personalities, but have taken to drink in the first place in order to relieve the effects of severe external stresses. In that event, efforts at modifying such stresses may lead to therapeutic success. Far more often, however, it will be found that the patient's personality has itself played a substantial part in the development of the addiction, and that the stresses could have been weathered without resort to alcohol if the habitual reactions to difficulty had been of a more satisfactory kind. In other cases, the stresses may have lain almost entirely within the patient's own personality, in the form of disabilities or conflicts, which, for one reason or another, he may not have had a high enough morale to deal with.

The uselessness of attempting to dissolve difficulties with alcohol may profitably be discussed with intelligent and co-operative patients, and plans made for the adoption of more satisfactory attitudes. In fact, the treatment will call for some psychotherapy, the underlying principles of which are discussed at length in this book.

Carl Jung once stated: "the craving for alcohol is the equivalent, on a low level, of the spiritual thirst of our being for wholeness, expressed in medieval language: the union with God."

Today, there is real hope for the alcoholic; he is maintained by the combined strength of his group's aura, assisted by the miraculous work of the simple but powerful Flower Remedies prescribed for him as an individual and not for his condition. Finally, there is therapy available from the level of understanding which may gain social acceptance, if not of the alcoholic himself, at least of the real causes behind alcoholism, the hidden, but very real side.

Dr. Douglas Baker
B.A., M.R.C.S., L.R.C.P.
England, 1977

Foreword

My name is David Lane, and I am a recovering alcoholic. I began to say this about twelve years ago when alcohol ceased working for me. I seemed no longer to be able to derive from it the benefits of inebriation and the temporary annihilation of unwanted feelings and thoughts of inadequacy that then plagued me. The sense of disconnectedness and inability to accept the paradoxes of life returned along with the feeling of not truly fitting into any place or scheme of things.

When alcohol ceased being the powerful number which it had been for many years, I became like a man in the middle of the ocean with no life jacket. I was an exposed, live wire set loose in a world whose reality was not my own. Therefore, I could not accept it.

My relationship with Bacchus ended; I began a journey on which I have experienced an unexpected reality of Self. There followed a further demand for Self-discovery, a thirst to serve others and insurmountable joys which the new understanding and acceptance afforded me.

Today I am faced with the challenge of risking that which I thought I knew, in order to experience with an open mind and heart, the multifaceted world of both the outer and the INNER Self. The prospect remains exciting.

I have not always accepted shifts in consciousness humbly or gracefully...nor have I experienced a continued state of bliss or Nirvana since I stopped using chemicals (alcohol) in search for the deeper meaning of Life. What I have come to know and to work with is a deep longing to connect, to realise a sense of spiritual wholeness after the fragmentation of my earlier years.

Also, what I am experiencing continually is a gradual awakening, an emerging into my awareness of a substance rich in the fundamentality of Life.

Six years ago, I came upon Dr. Baker's book *Alcoholism* (one of his many publications). This work, however, in view of my situation, caught my attention first through a friend in California who was a student of Dr. Baker's College and its correspondence course.

This friend, recognising my longing to go beyond merely 'putting a plug in the jug', offered me the possibility of searching deeper into my origins to discover the relationship of Man to the Universe and, through this expansion of awareness, to reach all other living creatures. This has changed my life.

For the past three years I have been studying Dr. Baker's works through his correspondence course.

What the book *Alcoholism* has given me, is a better understanding of what happens, what it was that I had been searching for all those inebriated years and it has given me a better perspective and a brighter attitude towards the world around me.

It is simple if I know myself and that I no longer need to accept what previously isolated me. I accept that there are things I don't know, and that which I don't know, I just *don't know*. I do know that my search is not at an end but I am already freer to choose more continuously my responses to the world about me.

Dr. Baker's book *Alcoholism* speaks for itself. It is anatomically and esoterically revealing, on different levels, of the whole possible human entity.

I am honoured to have been asked to write this foreword to the author's most helpful work.

David Lane
July, 1990

CHAPTER 1

ORIGINS

Man began drinking alcohol a very long time ago on this planet, certainly before Atlantis. Thus, it was used mainly in Lemuria as a device for stimulating the body's mechanisms for adjusting to changes in outside temperature. The earliest man's homeostatic devices were immature; his skin was very thin and had not yet developed that richness of organelles by which it is now characterised. Its insulatory devices (e.g., subcutaneous fat) and its blood capillary shunts were poorly established and had to await the sympathetic nervous system and its co-ordination with the fast maturing central nervous system. Sensory organs for deferring and adjusting to heat and cold were disseminated in the skin very late and this need was met in the earliest men by the pineal gland acting on the hypothalamic regions of the brain. The thickening of the skin, its keratinisation to prevent water loss, and its incorporation of tactile and other sensory organs also came very late.

Yeast cells had always flourished, deriving as they do from the plant kingdom, and had been given a spurt by the advent of the angiosperms and their fruit-bearing trees about eighty million years ago. At about that time, Man (mainly those elements individualising on the Moon Chain) began to materialise the first elements of his physical structures.

The spiritual and etheric states of consciousness experienced during Man's inhabitation of the Hyperborean Continent (See *Anthropogeny*, also by the author) were progressively lost during his transition from a purely etheric being into one with an etherico-physical vehicle.

He fed, at first, on juices and fruits, and these, when accumulated and allowed to ferment, gave him an exhilaratory beverage which, in addition, provided him with semblances of his long lost, yet instinctual, memories of the ecstatic states in Hyperborea, where spiritual beings were almost as common as primitive ones.

They associated the two, and our present word 'spirits'—alcohol—is testimony of this, the 'gift of the gods'. It is perhaps too much to suppose, that in addition to the ordinary interpretation of the word 'alcohol', of Arabic origin, 'hol' once referred to the drinker being made 'whole', hence 'holism', or one with the gods, imbued with his lost nature: his spirit. To the primitive man, this is what drinking the beverage implied.

Much later, as Man began to develop his Solar Plexus Chakra, and, with it, his emotional nature, (a spiritual event for him at that stage of his development), emotional growth was stimulated by alcohol, reinforcing the concept of the beverage's spiritual qualities.

Today, for Man on the Path, orientation away from emotional license, into mental polarity is the order of spiritual things and alcohol, though it may bring vague surfacings of archetypal memories of past spiritual glories, is not, in any way, an adjunct to, or a passport for, spiritual advance.

Nevertheless, in the earliest days, alcohol was prepared by the priests and medicine men, and its consumption was always in ceremonial groups accompanied by appropriate rituals, invocations and incantations, led by the various tribal officials. Minstrels and reciting bards were meant to bring back memories of former glories; dancing by maids and youths reminded the more mature of the lost land between lives, where physical imperfections imposed by age, held no sway.

Drinking or toasting by warriors before and after a battle not only reinforced unity and gave the event dramatic overtones, but made good sense in terms of 'Dutch courage'. Without casting any aspersions on the courage of comrades in arms in the Western Desert in World War II, all would agree that the trucks of Palestinian wine or brandy were a welcome sight during the long periods of abysmal defeat before the final victory in the Desert; commanders, even under puritan-like Montgomery of Alamein, made sure they were given every opportunity to reach the war front.

After the war, there were brave attempts at maintaining a transient camaraderie through reunions reinforced with alcoholic excesses, but these were pale candles in the suns of wartime associations, and reunions of College classes and 'Old Boys' gatherings are no better. But they do illustrate the powerful persistence of an ancient tradition that elevated experiences are best cemented when accompanied by alcoholic intoxication.

In Greece, and later in Rome, orgies of drinking accompanied the rituals of the religious cults of Dionysus and Bacchus. These were certainly by no means haphazard and pointless events. The Master Robert Browning indicates that the use of the product of the vine in these sects, symbolised, by drunkenness, the esoteric knowledge that the Earth was tilted on its axis and that its motion occasionally wobbled. It is only recently that his knowledge has been shown to have had any significance.

The occurrence of ice ages, their extent and their time periods are related to these factors. Also, through drunkenness in others, the initiate was shown what lack of control looked like, and to guard against loss of balance, harmony and control; they were put to the test under the impact of alcohol. We shall observe the relevance of this information to our subject in due course.

The Dionysian cults were well aware that alcohol promoted this abreaction so precious and desirous to the disciple. It is worth considering the matter in some detail in order to understand the esoteric aspects of alcoholism.

An Atlantean Disorder

There is no doubt about alcoholism being a condition of weakness inherited from Atlantis. There are groups of Atlantean souls coming into incarnation together, and part of their mission is to reduce the karma of that great cosmic entity Who is using the Atlantean Root Race as His physical body of expression.

Many of us have physical bodies of Atlantean stock susceptible still to Atlantean disorders. The impact of stress in our present society brings out and shows up these Atlantean weaknesses.

CHAPTER 2

THE ALCHEMY OF ALCOHOL

Alcohol is chemically related to water through its hydroxyl (OH) group of atoms. Water, or H_2O, is better read as HOH, and is technically 'hydro-alcohol'. Like water, alcohol has some astounding and unique properties, and like water, large amounts of it are absorbed through the wall of the stomach directly into the blood. Oxygen on its own can also be absorbed by the newborn child through the wall of the gastric mucosa. Indeed, when infant Man was still grappling with the problems of oxygenation, thirty billion years ago, his stomach served him in good stead as an accessory lung, as well as an absorber of glucose juices and their ferments, long before the digestion of vegetables and fruits necessitated the lengthening of the intestine and its subsequent morphological diversification.

Ecstasy, as it is understood by esoteric science, results from sudden movements and influxes of energy in the etheric body and its aura. Alcohol provides the physical body with boosts of high calorific energy. It is a food, but a food that has almost twice the calorific value of carbohydrates and proteins. Only fats exceed it in this respect. But it is through its actions on the movement of the blood and, indirectly, the propulsion of prana throughout the brain and nervous systems that it consoles man, and it is through its removal of inhibitions that it exuberates him.

There are many popular fallacies about the action of alcohol. It does not **cause** hypertension, arteriosclerosis or cirrhosis of the liver. It is not a stimulant. It does not directly speed the heart rate or make you think more clearly, even at first.

Alcohol moderates the critical faculties of the brain and removes the vagal nerve action of slowing the heart rate. It becomes an instrument of Maya, part of the Grand Illusion that snares all men. It brings the effects of Maya right down into the body cells. We **feel** better for it and, therefore, **think** we are better for it. The desires for new experience, response, and security are all given freer rein but most especially the desire for recognition. It is a false elixir, a spurious philosopher's stone: "...the subtle alchemist that in a trice Life's leaden metal into gold transmute."

The euphoria that alcohol provides comes from believing you are better than you are when in fact, at least from a physiological viewpoint, you are becoming less and less competent in a huge range of faculties. No wonder neophytes of Dionysus and Bacchus were introduced to alcohol debauches and then, later, as sober novitiates, were shown the same revels from behind curtains to illustrate with sad emphasis what lack of control can do to the minds and actions of men. The implication was that all men are, to an extent, subject to Maya, and intoxicated by the material world.

Alcohol deadens the mind to mental pain, and the physical body to suffering. The emotions are given freer licence, but at the expense of the hard won gifts of refinement, poise and purpose. Vision and memory are impaired, the performance of the muscular system is lowered and centres of the brain progressively shut down. I still remember the horror I felt when swotting up the signs and symptoms of alcoholism when I was at medical school:

Blood concentration of Alcohol

A. 100 mg per 100 ml equals dizzy and delightful
B. 200 mg per 100 ml equals drunk and disorderly
C. 300 mg per 100 ml equals dead drunk
D. 400 mg per 100 ml equals death's door (respiratory paralysis)

The horror was for the memory of a war comrade who was found 'drowned' (the medical orderlies had said) in his own vomit—a far-too-willing candidate for category D.

The deadening of the body by alcohol to the effects of pain is the first indication that the etheric body is becoming 'thinned out' if not actually detached from the physical body. Not only is diminishing judgement impairing the efficiency of the body functions but there is literally less vital energy being made available to the physical organs, the muscles, nerves etc.

Paradoxically, the resulting condition allows the astral body to act almost directly upon the physical shell. Emotions are almost uninhibited. The alcohol has a grossening effect and, speaking esoterically, this means that the astral body gets closer to the objects of its desires. In fact, during the episode of drunkenness, the astral body becomes completely aligned with the physical body and even during sleep or alcoholic coma, cannot detach itself. We will note the importance of this phenomenon later.

Health Hazards of Alcohol

The burden of detoxification of the alcohol and its elimination is almost entirely placed on the liver which can dispose of about one ounce of alcohol per hour. Little or no alcohol is excreted by the kidneys or lungs. This places a heavy load on the liver and, what is more important, on the Solar Plexus Chakra, a centre that is already stimulated and out of control in most of humanity.

It is true to say that alcohol is a food of a high energy level which is completely without vitamins. But it is not true to say that the liver will not degenerate if the alcoholic eats enough other food containing a sufficiency of vitamins. The truth is that scientific evidence shows that alcohol effects every cell it comes into contact with. (*Scientific American,* March 1976.) This finding is quiet confirmation of an esoteric teaching of long standing that alcohol is a general poison, especially for Man on the Path. C.W. Leadbeater, the great theosophical clairvoyant of the early part of this century, could observe, clairvoyantly, the effects of alcohol on the body and taught, eighty years ago that it was indeed a poison. It was also he who taught that cigarette smoking was a health hazard, sixty years before the Royal College of Physicians issued the first official announcement that there was a correlation between cigarette smoking and lung cancer.

Leadbeater also observed the precincts of drinking houses from the level of the astral plane and the effects of astral forces and entities on alcoholic imbibers.

It is a pity that this brilliant clairvoyant's

observations have not been taken more seriously of late by the mediocre core of the Theosophical Society especially with regard to his and Annie Besant's work in the field of Occult Chemistry.

Alcohol and its Effects

The author was able to view the effects of alcohol on himself in the immediate post-war period. Even the light use of alcohol had to be abandoned when he began to tread the Path some forty years ago, or restricted to an occasional glass of table wine. Understanding alcohol's many effects with the help of his medical as well as his esoteric knowledge, he makes the following comments which may be of help:

1. *With even the mildest alcoholic consumption, there is inflammation of the gastro-intestinal tract which causes pain and diarrhoea.*
2. *Acidosis, malaise (discomfort, uneasiness and indispositon), and nausea with a pounding headache.*
3. *An exhaustion lasting as long as two days. The most distressing aspect of this is the loss of the creative faculty...felt as a sort of spiritual aridity as if the Soul had momentarily fled.*
4. *Increased activity of the Brow area, with auric sensations (similar to the period that precedes a migraine attack). Occasionally this period might bring on high spiritual experiences, often with symbols strongly relevant to the preceding 24 hrs.*
5. *Vivid dreams, especially before waking, of the 'warning' type...dreams filled with symbols of impending disaster.*

6. *Insomnia. A period of four hours heavy sleep after·drinking, then an insomnia that heralded the first symptoms of hangover.*
7. *A disgust welling up from a deep level of consciousness.*
8. *An exacerbation of hypoglycaemia attacks (discovered during early years of medical training).*

These, on their own, would be sufficient to accentuate the sensitivity of the alcoholic to inner experiences. When there is also instability of personality, the hypoglycaemia can enduce schizophrenic and paranoiac outbursts. I deal with hypoglycaemia in another work: *Karmic Laws Behind Disease & Rebirth.*

9. *With the disgust, there comes a catharsis; a surfacing of elements of the Dweller on the Threshold* at a time when the psyche is least ready or able to deal with them.*

(*See also *The Jewel in the Lotus,* pp155-159, *Meditation,* p268, p288 and *The Psychology of Discipleship,* pp15-20, 65-67, 231.)

CHAPTER 3

THE ESOTERIC EFFECTS OF ALCOHOLISM

It is well known that when a man treads the Path, all that is good and all that is evil rises in him so that he is forced into the mighty confrontation with those elements of his nature. Those which are involutionary, constitute the components of his 'Dweller'; those which are evolutionary, constitute fragments of his fast-coalescing 'Angel of the Shining Presence', who acts as his guardian of the door of initiation.

It will help the healer to review some of the problems encountered by the disciple in dealing with mental and emotional disorders of the lower triad, in a process known as abreaction.

> *"With his increased sensitivity, with his greater strength and with purpose and direction clear in his mind, the disciple accepts the challenge presented not only by surfacing memories and experiences of this life, but of previous lives, which together have formed his present dweller on the threshold of consciousness at this early stage of his discipleship.*

The dweller is a loathsome entity, its components are astral matter of the lowest orders. It preys on the neophyte, drawing its substance from him in times of fear, worry, horror and other negative thinking during which the astral body, not yet integrated, haemorrhages. The dweller forms a negative vortex in a force field of which the chela is the positive and donating pole. The dispatch of this entity comes when it is confronted and recognised for what it is. The flow of auric energies towards it ceases and from sheer strangulation it flags and withers.

But it is an entity and will fight back for its survival taking every opportunity to highlight any negative scene or emotion with its presence just at a time when the disciple is shifting his focus from the outer world to the inner.

It is finally replaced with the birth and steady growth of the 'Angel of the Shining Presence', representing structures in Atma, Buddhi, and Manas, being proressively built into the aura through the assiduous efforts of the disciple in meditation and through his services to mankind and his devotion to the study of the occult classics. This is the background for the would-be initiate. It involves the replacement of old codes of conduct, preconceived or established ideas that tyrannised the mind of the disciple from his earliest years and which have been consolidated by his religion and his education.

The individual's dweller is but part of the gigantic Dweller on the Threshold of awareness of **Mankind**. *He draws from the col-*

lective phobias, idiosyncrasies and thought-forms of mankind. In destroying his own dweller, he performs an act of service to mankind, for, in so doing, he has also reduced the potency of that huge planetary entity anchored to the lowest planes of the astral world. This dweller is part of the collective unconscious described by Professor Carl Jung."(*The Psychology of Discipleship*, pp15-17.)

Dr. Francis Merchant gives a fine exposition of the more esoteric aspects of the Dionysian philosophy as practised in ancient Greece:

"This small country has given the world a multitude of highly significant myths. Prometheus, Jason, Hercules, Theseus, Oedipus —all these names arouse meaningful associations. There is one Greek divinity, however, who is rather infrequently discussed although his symbol is greatly honoured in modern society. I speak of Dionysus, more commonly known as Bacchus, the god of wine. His modern followers seem to know little of the god to whom they pay homage.

Only a few stray incidents about Dionysus have come down to us. He was the son of Jupiter, the wine and the corn were sacred to him. Those who participated in the rites he instituted attained through ecstasy a sense of oneness with divinity. King Midas is also associated with this god. Having befriended Dionysus, the king was told to ask for anything he wanted. He expressed the wish that everything he touched might be turned into gold. The granting of this request brought Midas no happiness, for his very food became inedible.

Sailors who sought to sell Dionysus into slavery were turned into Dolphins. King Pentheus, who prohibited the celebration of Dionysian rites, perished in consequence of his opposition.

We are told that the Greek drama arose out of the Dionysian festivals. In the Eleusinian Mysteries, Dionysus played an important role.

Wine, money and dramatic conflict—enduring symbols through the centuries—are thus emphasized by these myths.

The intoxication of the grape is but a symbol of the bliss attending spiritual union. The physical exhilaration that comes from imbibing wine is but anticipatory of the exhilaration inspired by creative ideas.

Dionysus stands for the inrush of inspirational energy that breaks up established modes and patterns. Physical intoxication, like sex, is but the lowest rung of a great mystery. Expansion and union have different meanings at various points of the ascending spiral of consciousness. The intoxication of the soul is to that of the body what fire is to the shadow it casts.

Those who cannot resolve their conflicts at the level of the soul seek relief in the negative unity that resides in the forgetfulness of drink.

The heart of the drama is conflict—conflict that springs from man's sense of duality, of separativeness, of disjunction. Endlessly he suffers, ever seeking the resolution of his dissonance. In sex, he seeks union; in drink, expansion. Dionysus points to higher techniques for achieving a more refined expression of these impelling tendencies. Union with the soul and the expansion of consciousness resulting from self-forgetfulness are gifts of Dionysus that have not yet been generally accepted. In the drama we have man's attempt to objectify his conflicts in order that he might attain understanding. The rapture of the poet and the mystic is an expression of intoxication at a higher level of awareness.

King Midas, his mind centred on gold, could profit nothing from the god's bounty —nor can the king's modern successors.

The rites of Dionysus, it has been said, are still being performed today. His body—the corn—is eaten, and his blood—the wine—is drunk. The participants in the ritual, however, often know naught of the god they honor, nor of the spiritual correspondences to which the external symbols point." (*The Golden Hoard*, by Francis Merchant, pp253-254)

Now it has been said that the thirst for alcohol is merely an outward manifestation of an inner urge for spiritual union. To support this, Carl Jung himself pointed out that the Latin word for alcohol is *Spiritus*, and that it is identical to the same word in Latin used for the higher religious experience. Perhaps Professor Jung's letter needs to be quoted in full:

Kusnacht-Zürich
Seestrasse 228
January 30, 1961

Mr. William G. W----
Alcoholics Anonymous
Box 459 Grand Central Station
New York 17, New York

Dear Mr. W.:
Your letter has been very welcome indeed.

I had no news from Roland H. any more and often wondered what has been his fate. Our conversation which he has adequately reported to you had an aspect of which he did not know. The reason that I could not tell him everything was that in those days I had to be exceedingly careful of what I said. I had found that I was misunderstood in every possible way. Thus I was very careful when I talked to Roland H. But what I really thought about was the result of many experiences with men of his kind.

His craving for alcohol was the equivalent, on a low level, of the spiritual thirst of our being for wholeness expressed, in medieval language: the union with God.

How could one formulate such an insight in a language that is not misunderstood in our days?

The only right way to such an experience is that it happens to you in reality, and it can only happen to you when you walk on a path which leads you to higher understanding. You might be led to that goal by an act of grace or through a personal and honest contact with friends, or through a higher education of the mind beyond the con-

fines of mere rationalism. I see from your letter that Roland H. has chosen the second way, which was, under the circumstances, the best one.

I am strongly convinced that the evil principle prevailing in this world leads the unrecognized spiritual need into perdition if it is not counteracted either by real religious insight or by the protective wall of human community. An ordinary man, not protected by an action from above and isolated in society, cannot resist the power of evil, which is called very aptly the Devil. But the use of such words arouses so many mistakes that one can only keep aloof from them as much as possible.

These are the reasons why I could not give a full and sufficient explanation to Roland H., but I am risking it with you because I conclude from your very decent and honest letter that you have acquired a point of view above the misleading platitudes one usually hears about alcoholism.

You see, 'alcohol' in Latin is SPIRITUS, and you use the same word for the highest religious experience as well as for the most depraving poison. The helpful formula therefore is:

SPIRITUS CONTRA SPIRITUM

Thanking you again for your kind letter,
I remain
yours sincerely,
C. G. Jung.

(Letter quoted from *The Grapevine*, International Monthly Journal of Alcoholics Anonymous, Vol. 24, No. 8, Jan.,'68)

If this were entirely true of alcoholics, it would explain how the condition seems to develop inexorably where the lifestyle, the marriage, the occupation, the cultural pursuits, etc. do not allow the expression of the soul. The inflow of the spiritual waters is inhibited because there is no outflow for them, or inability to express them in an environment that is arid and stifling.

It does not mean that the alcoholic is uncreative; many are extremely so, but whether their soul's purpose is being expressed in their creativeness is another matter.

CHAPTER 4

SPIRIT'S INVOLVEMENT WITH MATTER

Sometimes the soul's purpose cannot be expressed because of the heavy weight of the karma the patient is bearing. Until this karma is relieved, soul expression will be nigh impossible.

Where this karma must be worked off or where the karmic condition is satisfactory but the patient is not expressing the soul's purpose, there will be a deliberate halting by the soul of energisation of its lower triad.

At a **very deep** level, the alcoholic will feel a break with a loss of spiritual contact. He will then enter a sine wave of progressive degradation from within and working outwards; it will be reflected in descending order from the spiritual level down to the physical body. (See illustration.)

A rehabilitated alcoholic, now esoteric, described the process to me as follows:

"It seemed to me as if the degeneration began deep down inside me and then showed mentally, emotionally, and finally set in phy-

sically. Somewhere along that descent, I began to drink with less and less control."

The Seven Stages of Involvement with Matter

Now, for the esoteric healer, this curve is profoundly important. It is typical of man's descent out of a spiritual and archetypal pattern into the outward shell of a materialised physical body. (See *Anthropogeny,* also by the author.)

Mankind has a heavy karma, and an immense spiritual purpose in the cosmic order of things, and to resolve this, he has to descend into matter to engage with material things in a material body.

Understanding this curve of descent is vital for comprehending the way in which an alcoholic may rehabilitate himself because cure involves a reversal of the arc. Resolution of the karma of alcoholism restores the ability of the vehicles (from the physical body inwards) to express, once more, the soul's purpose.

On the descending arc of alcoholism, there is diminishment of creative thinking, a mental abnegation of previous responsibilities, and a developing mental isolation.

At emotional levels, there is increasing shallowness of affect, a loss of feeling for cultural meaning and family bond. Energies which previously were directed into many drives are now being focussed on one: the satisfaction of the outward show of thirst for what has been lost in-

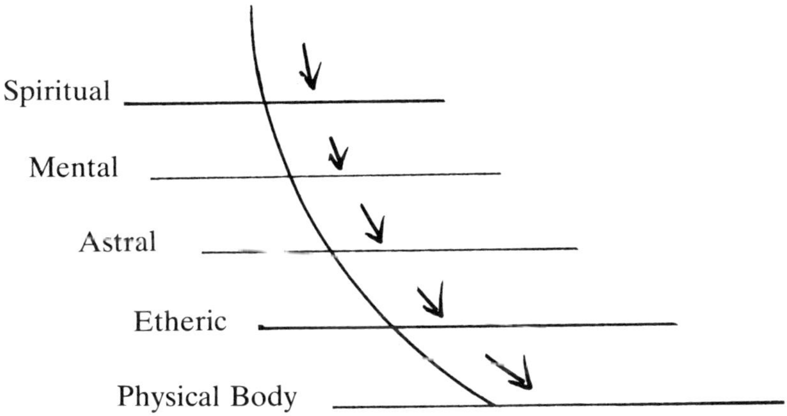
Spiritual
Mental
Astral
Etheric
Physical Body

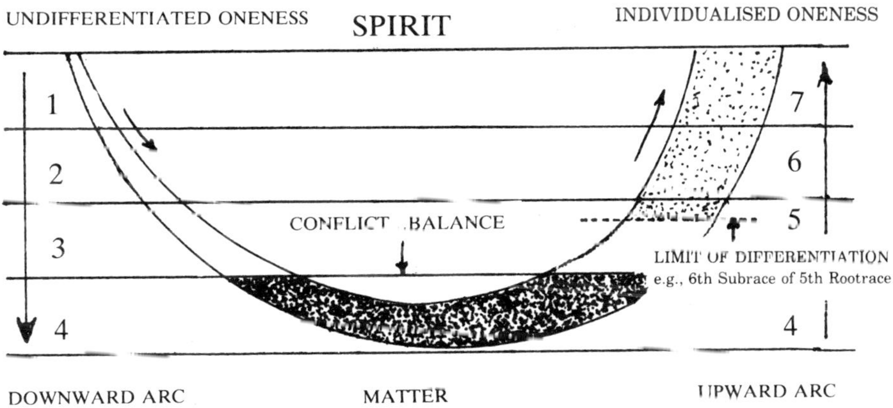
UNDIFFERENTIATED ONENESS
SPIRIT
INDIVIDUALISED ONENESS
1
2
3
4
7
6
5
4
CONFLICT BALANCE
LIMIT OF DIFFERENTIATION
e.g., 6th Subrace of 5th Rootrace
DOWNWARD ARC
MATTER
UPWARD ARC

Higher Mental and Spiritual Bodies
Astral Body (Emotional)
Physical Body
Etheric Body (Surround)

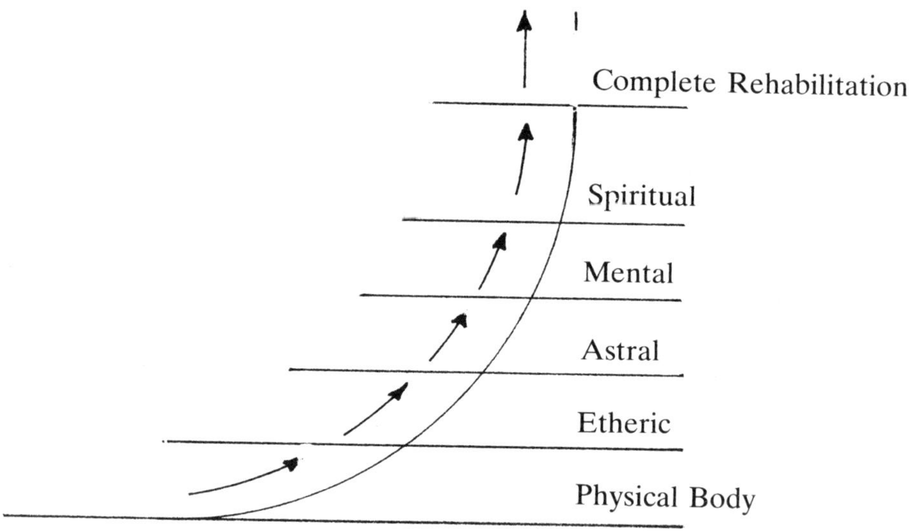
Complete Rehabilitation
Spiritual
Mental
Astral
Etheric
Physical Body

wardly. There are swings of mood, highs and lows.

When the etheric level is reached even these energies are dispersed. The vitality is diminished. Periods of complete exhaustion feature regularly. The subject is likened to a creature stunned. Finally, physical degradation begins. The features bloat, redden and hang, and the face is 'like the devil's, sick of sin'.

Then, at the rock bottom of degradation, all alcoholics agree about the occurrence of one supreme common experience: that of an overwhelming and nameless fear that besets them. The fear is so intense, so groundless, that some have described it as a 'fear of fear'. And only when this trough is reached, in which the most hellish experiences occur, with or without delirium tremens, can the process of the descending arc reverse itself, and the hard, upward struggle toward rehabilitation begin.

If therapists could understand the nature of this fear and its causes, the whole method of treating the alcoholic could be revolutionised and given a better chance of success.

The nameless fear that seemed to dog alcoholics at the point of their deepest involvement seemed to me to be a crucial factor in treatment. Whilst that fear existed, recovery seemed hopeless. It was this fear of he-knew-not-what that seemed to drive him back to the bottle. For my part, confronted over a period of five years with not a few friends in this horrible condition, I began to look into the whole phenomenon from the astral viewpoint.

CHAPTER 5

ASTRAL VAMPIRISM: THE HIDDEN SIDE OF ALCOHOLISM

My readers well know my book, *The Techniques of Astral Projection*, in which I teach methods of entering the astral world consciously and, once there, how to function helpfully on that plane.

The physical body is interpenetrated and surrounded by a force-field most generally called the *etheric body* or *etheric double*. This is a vehicle of subtle matter made of a material that interpenetrates any gas, liquid or solid just as easily as water interpenetrates sand. The etheric body has its own organs which are adequately described in any textbook on Theosophy.

It energises the physical tissues and, therefore, cannot be separated from the physical body for long. Dislodgement of the etheric matrix soon brings death to the overlying physical body. It cannot be projected.

Picture opposite: The Astral body out of alignment with the physical.

On the other hand, the *astral body* is projected almost every time we go to sleep. When we enter the sleep state we are usually still very active emotionally or astrally. We possess, as

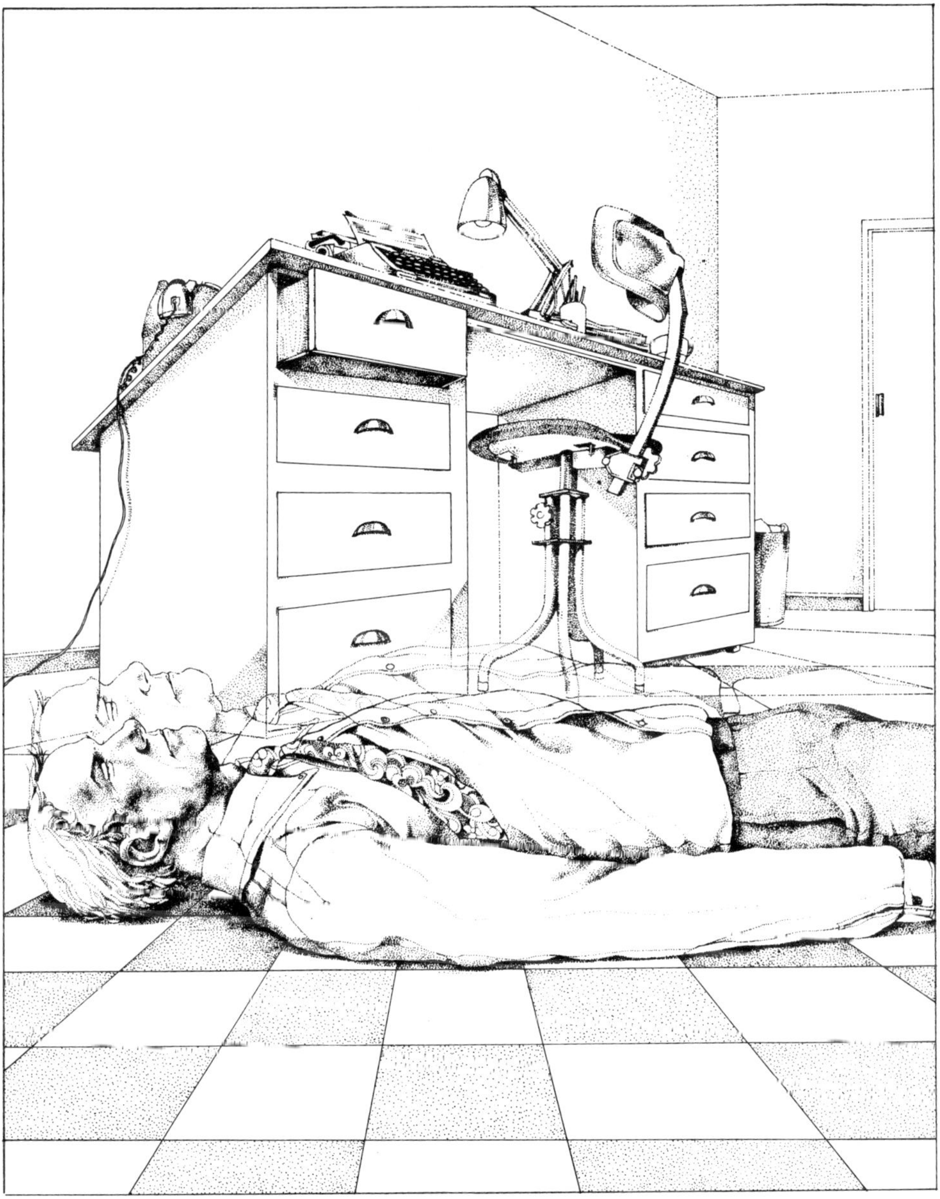

part of our normal equipment, both an emotional body which, in esoteric parlance, is termed the astral, and a mental body. These are both made up of matter even subtler than the etheric, already described. When we feel, we act in our feeling, or astral, bodies; when we think, we act mentally in our thinking, or mental, bodies. The astral body is made up of finer substance than the etheric body but not as fine a material as that of the mental.

In sleep, we slip out of the physico-etheric body and dwell in our astral and mental bodies. In these, especially the astral, we tend to move about in the astral world which is almost an exact replica of those places we visit in waking consciousness.

When we awaken, the astral and mental bodies slip back into their usual position in close alignment with the physical and etheric bodies.

For natural sleep to work its miracle of resuscitation, the astral body must go out of alignment with the physical. But in deep coma, such as produced by alcohol in any quantity, the astral body cannot leave the physical...cannot, in fact, come out of alignment with it. It is anchored to the physical body because of the massive metabolic activity going on in the liver, and because of the excessive stimulation of the Solar Plexus Chakra resulting from it. The astral body remains anchored to the physico-etheric body via the astral Solar Plexus Chakra.

I am reminded of an analogous process which occurs when monkeys are trapped by Africans. A hole is made in a melon or kalabash, just large enough to enable the monkey to insert his hand in search of melon pips. The trapper then rushes towards the monkey, who, in a panic, clutches the pips in his clenched fist with such determination that he traps himself. The monkey's clenched fist cannot be pulled out of the melon because the hole is too small...and he won't let go. Thus, he is anchored to the melon and easily caught.

By analogy, the astral body, in drunken coma, cannot let go of the physical body. Anchored to it, the individual becomes a target for astral attack. At first I could not believe the evidence of my own (astral) eyes.

Of more than a dozen examples of vampirism I have witnessed in alcoholics, the following was probably the most typical.

Gerald H. is a young man of very great sensitivity. Because of illness as a boy, he had fallen behind in his schooling and never really became literate. He was sensitive to this limitation. He blushed easily at the slightest stimulus and very frequently suffered from allergic responses. His face, arms and legs could swell rapidly in a few hours merely from 'his nerves', adding to his embarrassment in public. At first, he was wary of alcohol, especially beer, because it had led to enuresis, adding further to his sensitivity. Alcohol produced an 'allergic reaction' in him which he believed was related to gin, and then later to the lime juice he took with it. He had to be treated on several occasions for nervous spells. He was managing quite well as a butcher but then entered into a marriage which proved quite disastrous. She found him 'inadequate' and he considered her to be 'depressing'. She finally left him, removing all the furniture from the apartment whilst he was at work.

This further embarrassment proved too much for Gerald and his weekly 'booze-up' became almost a nightly affair. He would try to entice his friends to keep him company but inevitably went on the bottle alone. He would drink until the bar shut and then drive home to sink into a deep, intoxicated sleep.

At this stage, he came to me for help, though I had known him as a patient for many years. I quickly realised that his condition was serious; all the usual measures to help him desist were to no avail and to make matters worse, he lost his driver's licence through intoxication.

Because of his extreme sensitivity, and the accompanying tendency to cover up when questioned, I began to investigate him through astral observation. I had noted that he very rarely dreamed and slept more heavily than anyone I knew. One night, I was called by his landlady and told that he had drunk himself into a senseless condition.

During that night, I was able to project to him astrally. What I found in his presence confirmed my worst suspicions. As I approached him astrally, I could see that he was (astrally) quite conscious, but completely rooted to his physical vehicle. He was being attacked by discarnate alcoholics. Despite my many experiences of this phenomenon, I was horrified. He was screaming out: "No...no...no!" Two entities were clawing at his abdomen, in the region of his Solar Plexus Chakra. They were completely besotted, their eyes glazed and their mouths slobbering. They were literally drawing streams of white vaporous material from the navel area. I fought them off as long as I could, imploring Gerald to struggle out of his rooted position, his only chance of escaping from his assailants.

The following morning I called at Gerald's apartment. He was in bed, quite exhausted. He had absolutely no memory of any events during the night, nor did I expect him to have any recollection. He never did remember dreams or any events during sleep. It was quite useless telling him what I had observed. It would only have frightened him. I did suggest that when he was in such conditions, the very least he could do was to leave his bedroom light burning through the night, affording him some protection.

We now begin to understand something of the mechanisms at play in chronic and exacerbated alcoholism which make the recovery of the sufferer extremely unlikely. Drinking himself into a comatose condition makes him prey to astral attack. His emotional integrity, focussed in the nadis of his astral body, becomes sapped, persistently and exhaustingly, through astral vampirism.

He wakens with depleted emotional resources which makes the problem of rehabilitation all the more difficult. He has, through the night, sustained life in the astral world for a number of discarnate beings, still dominated by their lust and craving for spirits. The sudden or suicidal death of an alcoholic provides the most frequent source of astral vampires.

Discarnate Entities

The suicide rate of alcoholics is extremely high and the astral world has a high percentage of its population made up of discarnate alcoholics. Their numbers are excessive because, unlike other discarnate alcoholics, their worldly desires are, in most instances, unrequited. Suicide, an accidental death or death from some acute condition, like an overwhelming infection, does not bring an end to the desire nature...far from it! The earthly desires, after a short period of quiescence, reassert themselves in the astral body after death and the urge for drink, or to return to gluttony or sexual excesses surface once more into the consciousness of the recently dead.

The degree to which the vampirism may be taken depends on many factors. A chronic alcoholic might become the sole source of support for a discarnate being. The constant supply of alcoholic 'fumes' at an astral level, could maintain an obsessing entity for such a length of time that the consciousness of that entity could become merged with that of the living partner.

Picture opposite:
Astral Vampirism.

These effects were spectacularly described by the clairvoyant C. W. Leadbeater, who on

many occasions personally witnessed the crowding of astral entities, previously alcoholics, round bars, taverns and inns where alcohol was being consumed. It was as if something of the fumes, if not the actual liquid, could be drawn into their astral bodies at these sites.

The significance of these features of the astral life of these discarnate alcoholics has escaped the attention of those who deal with alcoholism in everyday life. It would have seemed unremarkable to the author as well if it were not for his researches into the factors restricting recovery of alcoholics who had come to him for help.

CHAPTER 6

HALLUCINATION AND POSSESSION

This obsessing is not confined only to alcoholics. There are 'demons' for every type of psychiatric condition. Very recently, the truth of obsession and its implications has engaged the attention of very orthodox and established practitioners:

> *Sri Rama, Moses, Buddha, Jesus, Muhammed—taught us as fact that human beings are subject to attack and invasion by hostile spiritual beings, beings which are utterly real, which have their origin outside the individual, and which can deeply affect and, under certain conditions, completely take over control of their human victims. At the same time, these teachers have taught that every man and woman is under the influence of utterly real, objectively existent heavenly beings.*
>
> *Most modern men simply do not believe this, and they do not at all recognize its connection with mental illness. Modern incredulity of the reality of spirits is powerful and pervasive. Every one of us is*

affected by it to some degree. We are programmed to disbelieve in spirits. Modern religions should serve a deprogramming function, but, with few exceptions, they do not. People may call themselves Christians or Jews or Buddhists or Muslims. But most of them—if they are 'civilized' and especially if they are 'well-educated'—have somehow managed to explain away or conveniently ignore what their religions' founders taught about the spirit world.

To those concerned with effective treatment for the mentally ill, it makes an enormous difference whether the modern or the traditional view of the spiritual world is the right one. It is obvious that proper therapy for a spirit-invaded person would be very different from treatment for a person who was just imagining things.

What if it turns out that there really are spirits and they really do affect human beings? What if the view which takes into account the existence and influence of spirits turns out to be valid? What if existence and Christ and Buddha and Rama and Muhammed and all of the other teachers were right? In that case, much of modern psychological theory would need to be reconstructed from the ground up. (24 *Magazine* Oct.'76)

Out of my professional role as a clinical psychologist in a state mental hospital and my own personal interest, I set out to des-

cribe as faithfully as possible mental patients' experiences of hallucinations. A discovery four years ago helped me to get a relatively rich and consistent picture of the patients' experience.

Though I noticed similarities with Swedenborg's description of the relationships of man to spirits, it was only three years after all the major findings on hallucinations had been made that the striking similarity between what twentieth-century patients describe and Swedenborg's eighteenth-century accounts became apparent to me. I then collected as many details as possible of his description. I found that Swedenborg's system not only is an almost perfect fit with patients' experiences, but even more impressively, accounts for otherwise quite puzzling aspects of hallucinations. I will first describe how I worked and then relate this to Swedenborg's work.

All the people involved hallucinated. They included chronic schizophrenics, alcoholics, brain-damaged and senile persons. The subjects of this study came to the attention of friends of the public because of unusual behaviour.

The average layman's picture of the mentally ill as raving lunatics is far from reality. Most of these people have become entangled in inner processes and simply fail to manage their lives well. In the hospital most have freedom of the grounds and the average visitor is impressed that, aside from occasional odd bits of behaviour, the patients have most of their powers and appear like almost everyone else. Many return home in a month or two never to need mental hospitalisation again.

Some become so enmeshed in inner processes that they slip to lower levels of mental disorder. The most severe disorder is usually that of a person who sits all day involved in inner processes, who obediently obeys the request of hospital staff to dress, eat, bathe, sleep in the hospital routine.

In many, even unusual beliefs would not be apparent. Most conceal that they hear and see things because they are wise enough to know the visitor doesn't and wouldn't understand. Their adjustment within the hospital is relatively good. Many do productive work ten to thirty hours a week. It is when they return to the relatively complex and demanding outside world that their adjustment worsens. None of the patients at the most severe level of mental disorders could be included in this study because they couldn't describe their hallucinations well enough.

After dealing with hundreds of such patients, I discovered about four years ago that it was possible to speak to their hallucinations. The patient was told that I simply wanted to get as accurate a description of their experiences as possible. I held out no hope for recovery or special reward.

It soon became apparent that many were embarrassed by what they saw and heard and hence they concealed it from others. Also they knew their experiences were not shared by others, and some were even concerned that their reputations would suffer if they revealed the obscene nature of their voices. It took some care to make the patients comfortable enough to reveal their experience honestly. A further complication was that the voices were sometimes frightened of me and themselves needed assurance. I struck up a relationship with both the patient and the persons he saw and heard. I would question these others directly, and instructed the patient to give word-for-word account of what the voices answered or what was seen. In this way I could hold long dialogues with a patient's hallucinations and record both my questions and their answers.

My method is that of phenomenology. My only purpose was to come to as accurate a description as possible for the patient's experiences. The reader may notice I treat the hallucinations as realities because that is what they are to the patient. I would work with a patient for as little as one hour or up to several months of inquiry where the hallucinated world was complex enough.

On several occasions I held conversations with hallucinations that the patient himself did not really understand. This was espe-

cially true when I dealt with what will be described later as the higher order hallucinations which can be symbolically rich beyond the patient's own understanding. There was great consistency in what was happening to them. The differences among the experiences of schizophrenics, alcoholics, the brain- and senile were not as the similarities, so I will describe these hallucinated worlds in general.

One consistent finding was that patients felt they had contact with another world or order of beings. Most thought these other persons were living persons. All objected to the term hallucinations. Each coined his own term, such as The Other Order, The Eavesdroppers etc.

For most individuals the hallucinations came on suddenly. One woman was working in a garden when an unseen man addressed her. Another man described sudden loud noises and voices he heard while riding in a bus. Most were frightened and adjusted with difficulty to this new experience. All patients describe voices as having the quality of a real voice sometimes louder, sometimes softer than normal voices. The experience they describe is quite unlike thoughts or fantasies. When things are seen they appear fully real." (*Hallucinations as the World of Spirits*, W. Van Dusen.)

To what extent astral possession occurs in the alcoholic during extreme distress must be a matter for further research. Certainly, two basic characteristics of alcoholism are described as a physical compulsion, coupled with a mental obsession. Both of these could be easily maintained by a possessing entity, if not actually evoked by it. It would explain, in the absence of any biological or genetic factor, the distinct physical desire to consume alcohol beyond the capacity to control it and in defiance of all the rules of common sense. Many alcoholics have, previous to their affliction, demonstrated immense talent and all the indications of will and those qualities attributed to a cultured and integrated personality. Only the invisible, but very real, intervention of some other 'personality' influence could account for the erosions of the alcoholic's character that occur with such dramatic and speedy certainty once rational incentives are swept aside.

Possession in these circumstances may not even be dramatic but might show up as foibles in character that could be overlooked unless the previous integrity of the alcoholic had been known. The qualities of possessing astral entities fit almost exactly the weaknesses of chronic alcoholics. The following comments by Swedenborg on the nature of 'spirits' incorporates many factors which could be equally observed in an alcoholic:

> *"When spirits begin to speak with man, he must beware lest he believe them in anything; for they say almost anything; things are fabricated by them, and they lie; for if they were permitted to relate what heaven is, and how things are in the heavens, they would tell so many lies, and*

> *indeed with a solemn affirmation, that man would be astonished...They are extremely fond of fabricating, and whenever any subject of discourse is proposed they think that they know it, and give their opinions one after another, one in one way, and another in another, altogether as if they know; and if a man listens and believes, they press on, and seduce in divers ways.*

Delusional ideas are common among alcoholics, and always present, according to Swedenborg, in spirits.

When sober, the brain of the alcoholic begins to function once more using rational mechanisms. It is only this, the physical brain when sober, that prevents a complete takeover of consciousness by an astral entity, for the latter lacks a physical brain with its memory components and its analytical and initiatory properties.

I would go so far as to say that, karma aside, alcoholism is almost entirely an astrally provoked condition made possible by the habitual disfunctioning of certain brain areas, especially those concerned with inhibitory factors. The dislocation of such areas permits infiltration of consciousness by astral entities and this leads to chronic alcoholism.

Delirium Tremens

The matter of delirium tremens now becomes explicable. There is no question here as to whether physical pathology is involved. The physical deterioration of brain tissue is responsible for many of the condition's symptoms—the raised temperature, the shaking of the limbs, the epileptic-like convulsions, all confirm this. What is of esoteric concern in the phenomenon is the acute hallucinatory aspects of the delirium. One has only to question an alcoholic about his visual experiences during the delirium and you will find that he is convinced that what he saw was real. The men that assaulted him and persecuted him were **real**. So were the snakes, and rats and insects he saw...as real as anything could be in his life.

The esoteric sciences confirm that there is abnormal but very real perception on the part of alcoholics in delirium tremens.

The effects of the alcohol have not been confined to the physical body. There can occur an abnormal arousal of two chakras; one of them, the Ajna, or brow centre, produces clairvoyance with perception in the lowest mental planes. The second chakra that is affected, even more easily than Ajna, is the Solar Plexus Chakra.

Pathological arousal by alcohol of this basic centre of the emotions leads to unavoidable visual confrontations with the denizens of the astral world. These visual experiences result on the one hand from a wearing through of the etheric webs that separate the chakras from each other, thus giving the normal energies of the etheric spine a freer passage for their tidal flow upwards. On the other hand, the chakra in the brow becomes excessively stimulated by the alcohol on its own whereas the safe process in Yoga is to open the three head centres simultaneously.

Where there is also auditory 'hallucination' there is usually an over-developed throat chakra as well and prognosis is poorer in these instances.

Sexually-orientated Entities

The intrusions of sexually-orientated possessing entities are inevitable. Astral individuals with strong and unappeased sexual drives can only obtain full orgasmic experience in or through a physical body. Rooted to the precincts of the Earth, they will seek out any weakened brain, alcoholic or otherwise, and entice the possessed one into masturbation, endeavouring to share the act which cannot be had in full acuity in the astral world.

All men know that the male dream life is often filled with sexual themes. They also discover very quickly that the culmination of a sexual theme to its logical conclusion in orgasm and ejaculation cannot be accomplished *without waking*. The sharpness of sensory feeling on the astral plane of the dream world is nowhere near to the refined and exquisite capacity of the physical plane to feel. A man has to come through to physical wakefulness to complete his sexual experience.

This consideration is important because experimentors in astral projection report that if temptation is not resisted, there is a hasty return to the physical body. An example of this is quoted here from *Life and Action*.

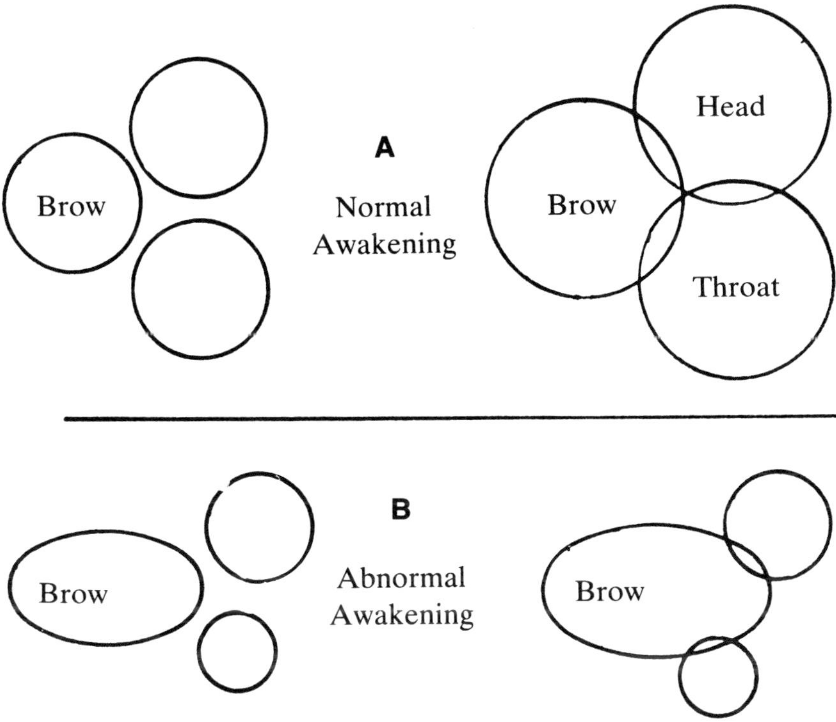
A
Normal Awakening
Brow
Brow
Head
Throat
B
Abnormal Awakening
Brow
Brow

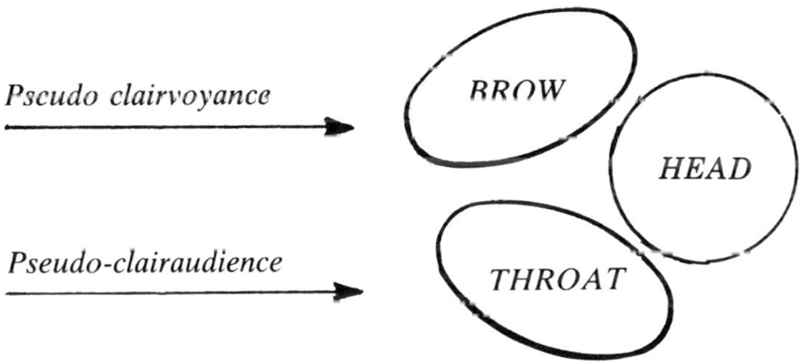
Pscudo clairvoyance
Pseudo-clairaudience
BROW
HEAD
THROAT

"In April, 1913, I was for about a month, Captain of the gunboat Marietta, and was lying alongside the dock in Brooklyn, N.Y. My wife remained at the house in the Naval Yard at Boston. One night I returned to the ship from the city, at about eleven o'clock, went to the cabin, and, in due time, retired to my stateroom and went to sleep in my bunk.

During sleep **I was conscious that I had left my physical body** *and travelled with seeming great speed over, but some distance above the ground to Boston, where I sought my own room and took my accustomed place in bed.*

Here, after a while, I was conscious that my wife had placed her hand on my shoulder, and I made a strong effort to turn over and respond to her touch. This effort seemed to cause me to leave the bed and room and return over the same route to New York at the same speed, and thereupon I reoccupied my bunk on board ship and awoke.

At once it occurred to me that this must be an **experience**, *so I reached out and switched on the electric light and noted the exact time. The next day I wrote to my wife without telling her anything about my experience, I asked her if she had noticed anything during the night in question.*

Her reply was that she strongly felt that I was in bed and had reached out and touched me on the shoulder! So real did it seem to her that she sat up to investigate, and finding nothing thought nevertheless that she would make a note of the time, which she did, and the two times, hers and mine, were identical." (*Astral Projection*, by Oliver Fox, aka. Hugh Callaway)

Both Sylvan Muldoon and Oliver Fox describe how, yielding to the irresistible temptation (irresistible, at least to their astral forms) to attract the attention of a charming lady, had sent them hurtling back to their physical moorings. (See *The Projection of the Astral Body,* by Sylvan Muldoon, London, 1929, 1939, 1950, 1961)

What are the components of the actual 'hallucinatory' experiences?

1. Elements of the Dweller on the Threshold, the individual's part of the collective unconscious.
2. Lower mental devas, and the myriads of components associated with the lowest of mental thoughtforms, like aggravation, torment, irritability, fear, disapproval, etc.
3. Elements of the lowest planes of the astral, the so-called purgatory and limbo. Animal and insect forms are mostly derived from the astral jungles of the lowest planes, some of which reach below the surface of the Earth. (See *Anthropogeny* pp 94-95)
4. Possessing entities (described above) and including succubus, incubus, sexual perverts etc.

5. A degree of irritation of the cortex of the brain caused by toxic effects of the alcohol and metabolic disorders resulting from it.

This is a horrible subject but no more horribly described than as it exists for the alcoholic in delirium tremens.

We must now consider the Soul's intent. What conceivable good can come out of a life given to alcoholism?

Many of the answers given here may themselves have therapeutic value in the treatment of an alcoholic especially where he has shown interest in esoteric matters.

CHAPTER 7

THE KARMA OF ALCOHOLISM

All individuals, somewhere in some life, have had to face the problem of alcoholism—have been tested with it and found wanting. There is no field of human experience in which the Monad will not plunge its lower triad; for it is in **overcoming** every aspect of material enmeshment that the Monad gains spiritual staying power.

The drives of many individuals are so varied and intense that the call of the Soul, the voice of conscience, cannot be heard. When these circumstances consume life after life, the Soul may choose a life in which all the drives are focussed into one overweaning and all-consuming desire: i.e., for alcohol. This concentration of a host of spread-eagled drives into one, makes the Soul's task easier. It reduces the number of lives needed to break the hold which the glamour of sensory and material matters have on its lower triad.

The Need For Attention

In previous lives, the alcoholic has held high ranking positions in society. There he has been the cynosure of all eyes...praised, adored, even hero-worshipped. But he abused his position. Instead of providing an example—a leader to his people—he became englamoured. He was too distracted by his own station, its dramatic appeal, by the sensory thrills it provided, the security and the elevation of stature. He failed to put his rank and position to good effect...ignored the sufferings of the masses, the appeals of the weak and voiceless. Instead, there developed a thirst for power, almost a megalomania.

John Richardson—Shakespeare—(See *Shakespeare: the True Authorship*, also by D. Baker) said there is one law for man and another law for the very beautiful. Like many beautiful people, these englamoured leaders abused the law and later are faced with the karma of their actions. Many beautiful people use the law justly and wisely, others abuse it. It is so very true of this karmic group: powerful people who abused their stations and have to pay for that corruption in later lives as alcoholics. But why as alcoholics?

In this life, the alcoholic again becomes the focus of attention; but now it is for different reasons. Now he is the cynosure of all eyes because of his debasement of himself. He becomes a mark for ridicule, disgust and scorn. In his intoxicated state, he often acts out his elevated and pretentious opinions of himself, his megalomania, his grandiose schemes and attitudes. But now no-one is fooled by such charades. The pendulum has swung to its opposite..."Vengeance is Mine, sayeth the Lord."

Karmic Results

There are as many karmic results of alcoholism as there are misdemeanors committed under its influence. Perhaps the most relevant to our times is the karma of drunken driving. I asked the Master Robert Browning to give me a visual image of the karma that results from the irresponsible actions of a driver who drinks without any regard for those who might be menaced by his resulting incapability.

As always, in such visual impressions flashed from the mind of the Master, you yourself must play the central figure, not a very encouraging experience when you are asking for visual impressions during occult research into the causes of such illnesses as rheumatoid arthritis and cancer, but it is all part of the Path of Sacrifice, which we must all tread sooner or later. In the vision that follows, I had to play the central figure, the dramatic 'I':

> *I was standing on a hillside looking towards my left at a freeway in the distance. A group of children were standing on the kerbside, wanting to cross the road. They correctly looked towards their right and then to the left to make sure no vehicles were coming, then held each other's hands and began to move quickly across the highway. Suddenly an automobile appeared, coming rapidly over the brow of the hill, and descended upon the group of children at break neck speed. Terrified, they scattered, but to no avail. The car bore down and ploughed into them. I was horrified.*

The scene faded and then resumed. Now there was the sound of a train's whistle in the distance. I looked over to the right and saw there was a great curve in the railway line down in the valley. From the curve, the line crossed a bridge. I could see that the train was travelling much too fast to take the curve. The engine driver was drunk. The train plunged over the edge and into the deep ravine below. Screams from the trapped and from the dying reached me. I ran down towards the wreckage. The carnage was awful. Between the dust and smoke I could see men tearing at the wreckage; the critically injured lay everywhere.

Suddenly everything went silent. And in the awful hush I found that everyone was staring at me. I stopped in my tracks and cried, "What's the matter?" There was a pause, and then someone faltered, "You are the only doctor here. You must take charge." I was stunned. I had no drugs, no surgical instruments...nothing. The responsibility of my position was appalling. I was the cynosure of all eyes. I was crushed by the weight of my circumstances as men and women and even trapped children cried to me for help.

This is the karma that results from drunken driving. In lives to come, such transgressors will be faced with situations of tremendous responsibility, responsibilities beyond their means, in which they will be given the opportunity to 'work off' the karma of irresponsibility which they evoked during their episodes of drunken driving in the earlier life.

Therapeutic Effects of Responsibilty

It is hard to suggest that the shouldering of responsibility be a part of the therapy for rehabilitated alcoholics. Heaven knows they have enough to contend with as it is. But where there is esoteric understanding, where spiritual strength is returning, this should be part of the rehabilitation: to shoulder responsibilities for mankind beyond that which normally faces a sensitive being. In simple words, the best therapy of all should lead to discipleship, to concern for the welfare of others, to sharing responsibility for the planet. This is the way of the disciple.

But, of course, this is exactly what Alcoholics Anonymous asks: that those who are rehabilitated help those who are still struggling.

The Factor of Love

Apart from the karmic factors already presented above, there is a basic underlying weakness in alcoholics. It is more of a blockage of energy than a lack of it. The alcoholic needs, and needs to manifest love.

To illustrate this point, I present here a passage from my journal, *Aquarius Rising*, dated February, 1959:

> *"This is the story of Mickey. It is told by Margeret who is my sister, for Mickey was her dog and it was she who had to make the*

decision, not an easy one to make either, when a man's life hung in the balance. My part in the story is only to record it here and to confirm that it is true, and that some of those concerned were my acquaintances, dispersed, but still in public life.

'Mickey was a canine of the '57 Varieties-type; he was presented to my one year old son when he was six weeks old. Unable to walk, he was the runt of a very poor litter, and his owner was quite sure he would never survive. The constant companion of my small son, he survived after much loving care and finally emerged from his mixed inheritance to be the healthiest and sturdiest little Scotty you ever saw, the only one to survive from the litter of five.

'When my son was five years old, we moved from the coast to Durban (South Africa) to stay with Molly, a very great friend who had a little girl of six. Mickey was very fond of riding in the car with us; he was always the first in and we never went anywhere without him. One day, Molly's husband Charlie went into town and of course Mickey went with him. It was already late in the afternoon when Charlie visited the butcher in the centre of Durban and, as usual, Mickey jumped out and followed. Upon returning to the car Charlie drove off, never thinking to ascertain whether Mickey was already in the car. When he arrived home we asked him where Mickey was, and he drove straight back to look for him, but the dog could not be found.

'We searched and advertised everywhere, with no result. For weeks we kept in contact with the S.P.C.A., but there was never a sign of Mickey. My son, an only child, was heart-broken at the loss of his constant companion, and even today, twelve years later, still talks of him.

'But there is a sequel. Months later, Molly and her daughter stopped at a tearoom in Pinetown, a village just outside Durban. All of a sudden the little girl was screaming wih delight; a little black dog was prancing all over her. Both at once recognised Mickey and Molly asked the proprietress of the tearoom whether she knew who owned him. She was told that he belonged to a man who worked at the ——Insurance Company, but who lived up the road. The Manager of the Insurance Company was a personal friend of ours, and later Molly called on him to ask if there was anyone employed at his company who possessed a Scotty dog. She was told that this was the case: the man concerned was so devoted to it that it was his constant companion; he even brought it to work with him. He denied Molly's claim to the dog and I was called in to identify him. Mickey had been run over as a pup and had a scar on his groin. By this means I was able to prove that he was one and the same dog, and our friend, the Insurance Manager insisted the dog be handed over. My son's joy knew no bounds when we brought him his 'Mickey Moo' home!

'Some months later we had a visit from a Mr. McGregor, Chairman of the local Alcoholics Anonymous. He pleaded with us to give the dog back to its erstwhile owner at Pinetown, who was in such a shocking state that they feared for his life. This sounded a bit far-fetched. As I said before, my son was an only child and I was loathe to deprive him of his playmate for the second time for obvious psychological reasons. I refused.

'A week later, Mr. McGregor was back, begging me to reconsider. He told us that the man was **dying.** *This was hard to believe so we went to Pinetown to see for ourselves. I shall not easily forget the change that I saw in that man. He was lying on a divan in the verandah in a shocking state. He looked like a corpse; there was just no will to live. The A.A. had bought him a fox terrier, of which he took not the slightest bit of notice. The shaking hands sought only one thing, the bottle nearby. The A.A. had done all they could for him, but he only wanted Mickey. His story, pieced together by Mr. McGregor, was quite simple. He had been struggling for years with his problem and had recently had a bad bout. He was walking the streets one night and had found Mickey, very forlorn, leaning against a pole in the pouring rain. He had taken the dog home and from that time had pulled himself together, got himself a respectable job and become the respectable citizen he was when I first saw him at the Insurance Company with Mickey. I had to admit Mickey was in the best of condition*

when returned to us, and he must have looked after the dog very well.

'Never again do I want to face the decision I had to make then, between a child's breaking heart and a man's life. I agreed to part with Mickey once again.

'Today, Mickey's owner is in an executive position in Cape Town, fully recovered from alcoholism, through the love of a little mongrel. I had always been told that only love could cure the alcoholic; now, I know it.' "

The lessons from that true story are self-evident. But what of the *type* of love that is required by, and for, the alcoholic?

He must be taught not selfish, attaching love, but selfless love. Not an 'I-will-love-you-if-you-love-me-back' attitude, but an 'I-will-love-you-no-matter-what'.

Discrimination of the Real from the unreal, the assumption of responsibilities for others, the practice of compassion for all living things... these are the disciplines which could reduce the tremendous build-up of energies around the Solar Plexus Chakra of the alcoholic. If he, him self, cannot evoke these qualities from within, then the esoteric healer should apply them to the alcoholic. The stimulation of his heart region will ease the strains for him and loosen the grasp of possessive entities.

CHAPTER 8

PSYCHOTHERAPEUTIC TREATMENT

The alcoholic lacks the power to transfer energies from the Solar Plexus Chakra, which lies below the diaphragm into the Heart Chakra which lies above the diaphragm. The energies of the former are almost entirely emotional and attaching. Thwarted emotionally in his daily affairs, his attachments quickly centre on that which he can hold firmly in his hands, and which will substitute for him things that will replace the series of broken images, the idols he has erected for himself to worship at, which Life so rudely destroyed.

The great Master of the Wisdom and Lord of Compassion, K.H., Who, in His previous life was St. Francis of Assisi, used these words:

God grant me the serenity to accept things I cannot change
The courage to change the things I can,
And the wisdom to know the difference.

They have been adopted as the Serenity Prayer of Alcoholics Anonymous.

It is easy to understand why Alcoholics Anonymous is so successful. It incorporates so many aspects of the Ray of Love-Wisdom...its universality, its compassion, its service to mankind, etc. The esoteric student and healer would do well to ponder on its aims and methods:

1. Belief in God and **Natural Law**; compare this with Karma.
2. Frank **Self-appraisal**; meditation uses the same techniques.
3. Willingness to admit and correct wrongs done to others...facing the Karma of **this** life.
4. A trust in Mankind...concept of Universal Brotherhood.
5. Dedication to rescue those who sincerely desire to conquer alcoholism by making them members as successful abstainers. ...'Am I my brother's keeper?' To the esotericist, the answer is 'Yes!'

A.A.'s Group Psychotherapy

The system of its psychotherapy has rehabilitated more alcoholics than the combined resources of medicine, psychology and psychiatry. Motivated by the survival needs of its members rather than by the scientific curiosity of orthodox medicine or the blind discipline of a doctor-patient relationship, its greatest value lies in its group therapy treatment of the problem of alcoholism. A minority movement, seeking justice in a world that classes the alcoholic as deviant and immoral, AA gives the alcoholic what he has always wanted: social acceptance by a group that cares about him and understands him, especially at his lowest.

The outstanding qualities of the alcoholic at his lowest are: *wrong motivation*, everything is sacrificed for the binge; *separativeness*, he will drink alone, endlessly, and be hostile to non-alcoholics; *indifference, harmfulness, selfishness* and *ingratitude*.

All these are the very opposite manifestations of Love-Wisdom. The least the therapist can do is to prescribe the Flower Remedies for these symptoms. In taking a case-history before prescribing, the list given above (by no means complete) should aid the gentle enquiries of the therapist.

As we review the levels of disintegration which the alcoholic patient went through on his downward journey to his 'pit of hell', we are confronted with the soul condition, the mental condition and finally the physical level of his symptomatic list. Beginning with the process of unnamed fear, the Flower Remedy prescribed will be Aspen; Aspen for a person trembling with fright, especially a nameless fear, as most alcoholics will reveal, or even conceal, according to their temperaments. Also give the patient Agrimony for his craving for alcohol. The first condition of treatment is to stop the intake of alcohol completely, and Agrimony can help him in this most desperate struggle.

Emotionally, the patient will need the therapist's support, something to help rid that deep feeling of self-disgust, as if he wants to cleanse himself. Every human being, at some time or other has had experiences at a physical level when getting into a bath couldn't be quick enough; even air travel, crowded trains and buses can create such a desire. Crab Apple is the Flower Remedy to dispose of the feelings of guilt and self-disgust.

Then there is the etheric stage for the patient, the stage of physical exhaustion when his very life's blood seems to be drained from him, when nothing vital comes through the etheric matrix: the prana just cannot get through. Olive is the remedy for this physical exhaustion on the etheric level of his upswing.

Then for the despair, doubts, and depression which will invade the patient from the astral plane to undermine all his efforts toward rehabilitation, give him Gentian.

Then comes the mental level for consideration, where the negative conditions listed above will all be present in the case history. It is here that the therapist must begin to think of prescribing by a repertoire of remedies, i.e., a whole series for mental symptoms which are changeable in an individual and the changes are usually fairly frequent, especially in the alcoholic patient. Olive for the mental fatigue, Agrimony for the mental torture and Hornbeam for sustained mental effort. It is here that the Oak will assist the patient in his struggle against mental odds, the sort of odds that most alcoholics have to face when people around them say, "Oh yes, we've heard all this before," when he is desperately in need of their loving understanding.

At Soul level, at least six months after recovery, Holly is the recipe for Love-Wisdom and Sweet Chestnut, the remedy for anything related to the soul, like the 'dark night of the soul'. This brings the alcoholic back to the level where it all began: his Soul's desperate cry for recognition and expression.

But now, at least, there is real hope for him; he is sustained by the combined strength of the group's aura, assisted by the miraculous work of the simple but powerful Flower Remedies prescribed for him as an individual and not for his condition. Finally, there is therapy available from the level of understanding which may gain social acceptance, if not of the alcoholic himself, at least of the real causes behind alcoholism.

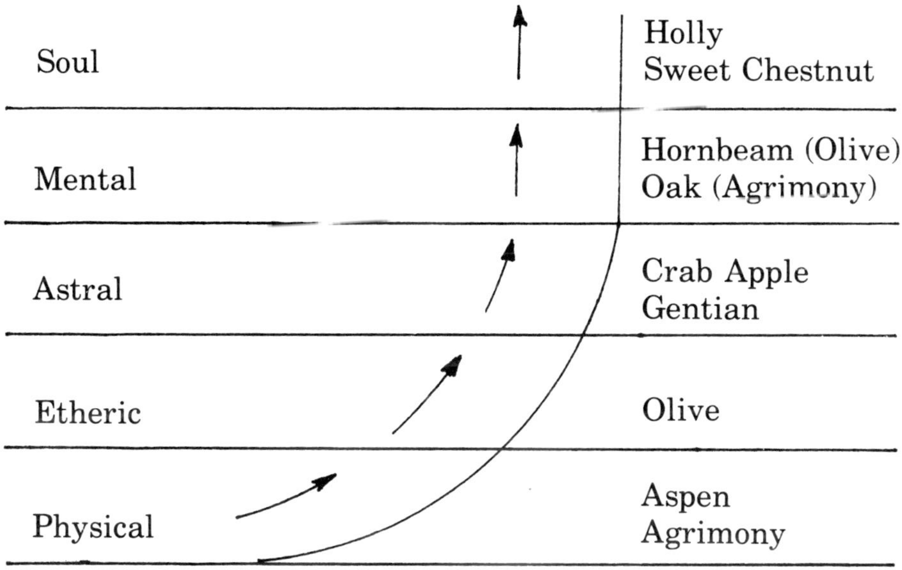

Soul
Holly
Sweet Chestnut
Mental
Hornbeam (Olive)
Oak (Agrimony)
Astral
Crab Apple
Gentian
Etheric
Olive
Physical
Aspen
Agrimony

CHAPTER 9

PROTECTION AGAINST VAMPIRISM

How can the solar plexus region be protected from vampirism which causes the lack of desire to resist? This is a field of research for the future.

The use of physical devices may be effective if they produce material or forces which are etheric in nature. The possibility of using ionising equipment in the umbilical area suggests itself.

Any disturbance in the etheric field of man will set up repercussions in the astral body. The electron is the first basic unit of the first plane of the etheric and ionised particles are representative of the lowest subplane of the etheric. Negative ions have long since been known to be therapeutic for man in many fields, especially in very sensitive conditions like asthma which have psychosomatic relationships. The advent and development of Kirlian photography by the Russians has shown man to have a 'bio-plasmic body':

> " '*As if there issued forth from canals in the skin, cold, powerful flames, furiously flash-*

ing solar prominences, an entire herd of 'amoeba-like' lights crept from place to place then formed into one blazing bonfire, then divided into pieces again.'

'A fire world.'

'Radiance like the Aurora Borealis.'

"These words were used by a group of Soviet scientists to describe the phenomenon they had just witnessed: it was the human body, seen in a field of high-frequency electrical currents.

"The Russians claim they have discovered a new form of energy, a biological energy, different from mechanical, magnetic or electrical forms; the term they have coined for it is 'bio-plasma'. They postulate the existence of a 'bio-plasmic body', which interpenetrates the physical body, and which they feel may be the underlying pattern which determines its physical shape." (Quoted from *Technical and Medical Research on the Negative Ion*, issued by the Life-Ion Corporation, Bloomington, California.)

It may well be that the application of high-frequency electrical currents to the solar plexus region (not to be confused with E.C.T.—electro-convulsive therapy) could be monitored by conscious mediums able to view the process astrally. It would soon be discovered whether this could drive off possessing astral entities.

Certainly, the application of weak, pulsating

magnetic fields to chakra areas can raise their energy levels and offset vampirism, which is not confined to astral and discarnate beings. There are many very negative people in living flesh who sap energy from the solar plexus area of their friends, if not from innocent bystanders themselves! I, myself, on many occasions have had to wear a silver foil disc over the solar plexus to halt the transfer of energy to avid and depleted sappers during spiritual consultations.

Maintaining the comatose alcoholic in conditions of a brightly lit room, day or night, would cetainly convey some protection. The properties of physical light act sharply against any sort of concreting action by astral substance.

The whole matter needs research and there would be a need for capable astral observers to bring back objective information about protection methods employed.

It is far more likely, that negative ionisers, shaped as discs and strapped to the solar plexus region would be helpful. Corporations manufacturing and distributing these ionisers already exist, but they need to be used with caution.

There is no doubt that ions would affect the autonomic nervous system of which the Vagus Nerve is a part.

Effects of Therapy on the Brain and Nervous System

The most important related discovery may, however, be the direct influence of atmospheric ions on the autonomic nervous system, which is respiration and heart function. This system controls many of the automatic biological phenomena that take place in the body.

A most important neurohormone in this system is called serotonin, which is also found in the brain. An increase in the hormone may cause pain, cramps, irritability, insomnia, stress and general discomfort. Also, a feedback correlation exists between serotonin and many other hormones.

At the University of California and in Russian laboratories, the influence of positive and negative ions on blood and brain serotonin has been conclusively demonstrated:

A. Positive ions lead to increased release of serotonin which in turn brings on the conditions mentioned in the preceding paragraph.

B. Negative ions stimulate enzymes which destroy serotonin and bring about healthy conditions in the body and feelings of well being.

When environmental conditions do not allow negative ions to exist in sufficient quantity, serotonin production rises, accounting for adverse effects in the behaviour of sensitive individuals to weather changes.

Dr. A.P. Krueger, professor, University of California, Berkeley, who has studied air and gaseous ions for eighteen years, states that the cause of the poor and unstable psychic and physical conditions of many people today is due to the lack of balanced air ions in polluted cities. (*Technical and Medical Research on the Negative Ion*, Life-Ion Corporation, Bloomington, Calif.)

APPENDIX 1

KARMA

The term 'karma' comes from the Sanskrit word **Karman**, which is a noun-form from the root 'kri', meaning 'to do' or 'to make'. Literally, Karma means 'doing', 'making' action. But when used in a philosophical sense, it has a technical meaning, and this technical meaning can best be translated into English by the word 'consequence'. Thus:

> *"When an entity acts, he acts from within; he acts through an expenditure in greater or less degree of his own native energy. This expenditure of energy, this outflowing of energy, as it impacts the surrounding milieu, the Nature around us, brings forth from the latter, perhaps an instantaneous or perhaps a delayed, reaction or rebound. Nature, in other words, reacts against the impact of that energy, and the combination of these two, of energy acting upon Nature and Nature reacting against that impact of energy, is what is called karma, being a combination of the two factors. Karma is, in other words, essentially a chain of causation, stretching*

back into the infinity of the past and, therefore, necessarily destined to stretch into the infinity of the future. It is unescapable, because it is in universal Nature, which is infinite and, therefore, everywhere and timeless, and sooner or later the reaction will inevitably be felt by the entity which aroused it.

It is a very old doctrine, known to all religions and philosophies, and since the renaissance of scientific study in the Occident, has become one of the fundamental postulates of modern co-ordinated knowledge. If you toss a pebble into a pool, it causes ripples in the water, and these ripples spread and finally impact upon the bank surrounding the pool; and so, modern science tells us, the ripples are translated into vibrations, which are carried outward into infinity. But at every step of this natural process there is a corresponding reaction from every one and from all myriads of atomic particles affected by the spreading energy.

Karma is in no sense of the word Fatalism on the one hand, nor what is popularly known as 'Chance', on the other hand. It is essentially a doctrine of Free Will, for naturally the entity which initiates a movement or action, spiritual, mental, psychological, or physical, or other, is responsible thereafter in the shape of consequences and effects that flow therefrom, and sooner or later recoil upon the actor or prime mover.

Since everything is interlocked and interlinked and interblended with everything else, and no thing and no being can live unto itself alone, other entities are of necessity, in smaller or larger, degree, affected by the causes of motions initiated by any individual entity, but such effects or consequences on entities, other than the prime mover, are only indirectly a morally compelling power, in the true sense of the word 'moral'.

An example of this is seen in what the theosophist means when he speaks of 'family karma' as contrasted with one's own indiidual karma, or 'national karma', the series of consequences pertaining to the nation of whivh he is an individual, or again, the racial karma pertaining to the race of which the individual is an integral member. Karma cannot be said either to 'punish' or to 'reward' in the ordinary meaning of these terms. Its action is unerringly just, for being a part of Nature's own operations, all karmic action ultimately can be traced back to the cosmic heart of Harmony which is the same thing as saying pure consciousness-spirit.

The doctrine is extremely comforting to human minds, inasmuch as man may carve his own destiny and, indeed, must do so. He can form it or deform it, shape it or misshape it, as he wills, and by acting with Nature's own great and underlying energies, he puts himself in unison or harmony therewith and therefore becomes a co-worker with Nature as the gods are."

(Quoted from *The Occult Glossary*, by G. de Purucker, Theosophical University Press, Pasadena, California.)

APPENDIX 2

The following notes were taken from *Psychological Medicine* by Maurice Partridge and Desmond Curran. Though written some thirty years ago, their observations are as appropriate today as ever.

"The moderate consumption of alcohol is a normal social habit in most countries. This habit can be considered a medical problem only if: the amount of alcohol taken leads to symptoms which call for medical aid; the individual develops symptoms when the supply of alcohol is interrupted; or when signs of organic deterioration appear.

Acute Alcoholic Intoxication
The first signs are usually increased talkativeness and mild euphoria. These are evidence of disinhibition. They are succeeded by failure in concentration, with forgetfulness owing to defective registration of what is happening, followed later by frank impairment of memory, superficial thinking, irritability, and lack of judgment and insight.

People vary considerably both in their tolerance to alcohol and in the sequence in which the signs are shown. In some, physical signs such as slurred speech and other evidence of motor inco-ordination appear very early; in others mental signs alone may be observed until an advanced stage of intoxication has been reached.

Patients with cerebral disease or injury, specially those with epilepsy are liable to show severe signs of intoxication (drowsiness, irritability, excitement) after quite small doses of alcohol, and this is an important point to remember where there is some legal involvement.

Treatment

Cases may be encountered who show violence and uncontrollable behaviour under the influence of alcohol. Medical aid may sometimes be sought on this account, and this seems to have led to the formulation of a psychiatric syndrome, copied from from one textbook to another, and known as **mania a potu**, as though this were some disease entity on its own. Many cases of uncontrollable excitement (sometimes after only moderate doses of alcohol) have had nothing in common with mania, and the use of the above term is merely a source of confusion. Such cases may be regarded as explosive reactions, facilitated by alcohol in people specially susceptible to it, either innately or as a result of cerebral injury or in association with epilepsy; such people are commonly liable to show psychopathic behaviour whether drunk or sober.

The prime necessity in treatment is to secure

enough help to restrain the patient and to remove from the environment anything potentially dangerous to himself or to others. The excitement may then be reduced by the appropriate administration of certain drugs and very large doses of vitamins, mainly of the vitamin B complex.

Alcoholic Coma

All comatose cases require careful examination. It is unwise to attribute a comatose state to alcohol and to leave it at that, unless a definite history is established that will satisfactorily explain the condition on that ground alone.

The smell of the patient's breath is not necessarily a reliable guide, for people are often given brandy or whisky on feeling faint, but may have had no other drinks; and drunk people may sustain head injuries through falling, and may be diabetic. It is important also to exclude insulin coma, as the development of symptoms after an overdose of insulin may be very similar to that of alcoholic intoxication.

Treatment

The only immediate practical measure is to wash out the stomach, the contents of which can then be examined. So long as there is doubt as to the cause of coma, the patient should be kept under observation, with repeated attention to temperature, pulse, respiration, blood-pressure and the development of eye signs.

Acute Alcoholic Hallucinosis

This is a rare condition which generally starts after an excessive drinking bout. It may be the herald of delirium tremens. The predominant features are hallucinatory voices, commonly reproachful or threatening, experienced without much clouding of consciousness. The mood is usually one of fear, as in the full-blown delirium tremens, although traces of alcoholic jocularity may be observed. Some cases turn out be schizophrenics who have taken alcohol to drug themselves in the first stage of an acute schizophrenic episode.

Chronic Alcoholic Hallucinosis

This condition is also rare. It may develop after an acute hallucinosis, or it may be insidious in onset. In either instance it is characterised by numerous auditory halucinations in a clear setting and without much disturbance of behaviour. The voices are characteristically repetitive and rhythmical: 'idiot, idiot, idiot' or 'beggar, beggar, beggar'. The condition tends to be persistent and some patients get used to their voices and will carry on with their work in spite of them. More often, however, delusional misinterpretations occur as a result of the voices, and the patients become so paranoid as to require institutional treatment.

Alcoholic Paranoid States

Alcohol can play a part in the production of paranoid states that may have a close resemblance to paranoid schizophrenia, or, when a grandiose colouring is added, general paralysis of the insane, but carrying a much better prognosis. Important points to look for are: the history of alcoholism; a greater variability in the clinical picture than occurs in paranoid schizophrenia or general paralysis; organic mental features, e.g., difficulty in grasp. The differential diagnosis from general paralysis may only be possible after serological investigations; for example, slurred speech and purillary changes may be present in both.

Chronic Alcoholism

This may be considered established when a person habitually takes more alcohol than do others in his environment and becomes unable to do without it, so that his drinking is beyond control. The habit, once established, tends to be self-perpetuating, and if alcohol is consumed over long periods in large quantity, the individual becomes habituated to and physiologically dependent on it.

Aetiology

More commonly, the reasons for excessive drinking must be sought in the personality of the individual concerned, rather than in his own environment. Thus, many alcoholics are **psychopathic personalities**, as would be expected from our knowledge of the latter. In other people, not necessarily psychopathic, the tendency to drink excessively arises from **personal problems**.

In general, such problems involve frustration and dissatisfaction, and alcohol is resorted to because it is a powerful solvent of reality, for the time being. Common problems of this sort are domestic disharmony, homosexuality, failure to achieve ambition and to adjust to such failure, and a sense of social inferiority, which alcohol helps the individual temporarily to overcome. As a talented actor, whose wife was more successful than he, expressed it: "Once I'd had that failure it was difficult to meet my equals as I had before, and frankly I preferred to be cock of my own dunghill in the local." Such drinking comes under the heading of **neurotic reaction**.

Finally, excessive drinking may be symptomatic of some more definite psychiatric illness. The lack of restraint in early GPI or other organic deterioration may facilitate alcoholism. The same is true of recurrent hypomanic and depressive attacks, many of which are responsible for that tendency to recurrent and periodic drinking which is known as **dipsomania**. In such cases, a history of symptoms preceding the consumption of alcohol may be of diagnostic importance, particularly for forensic purposes.

Physiological Dependence

Why the person becomes physiologically dependent on alcohol once the habit is established is unknown. But such dependence is a far more real and serious matter than might be supposed. In the advanced alcoholic it is more than a question of weak will. As his drinking increases from the evening until it starts in the afternoon, and then in the morning and then before breakfast, the alcoholic knows that he is wreaking his own ruin. But more alcohol, and then more alcohol is necessary to control the symptoms that he feels when his intake is below a certain level. And the level is always tending to rise. It must also be realised that at a certain stage, one drink automatically and inexorably leads to another, just as the avalanche inevitably descends once the slip of the sustaining snow has started.

Symptoms and Signs

Owing to the defective judgement and deterioration that ensues from chronic alcoholism, as well as from its expense, all sorts of social and financial difficulties are liable to arise. The more insurmountable they are, the greater may be the solace that alcohol temporarily affords, so that a vicious circle is set up. Alcoholics tend, however, to be singularly deficient in insight, and cannot be convinced that their troubles arise from their habits.

Their lot is such as often to arouse sympathy. At the same time, many are 'men of the world' with remnants of a personality that was once engaging. This may lead them to show an apparent frankness, not without a spurious charm, but which is allied in fact to shamelessness. For these reasons, the doctor must be on his guard and should recognise, even if his fellow club-members do not, that when an inebriate claims to have put all his cards on the table, a number are probably face down.

As to physical symptoms, nausea and vomiting, especially in the morning, are often complained of and are due to alcoholic gastritis. Anorexia is usual, and of importance in that it helps to cause Vitamin B deficiency, which contributes to the clinical picture. Paraesthesiae and weakness are often complained of, secondary to peripheral neuritis.

As to signs, the first of ill-omen is liable to be a falling off in the patient's capacity to hold his liquor, or, when a patient, not overtly drunk, and apparently managing satisfactorily, is found to have an amnesia for what he has been doing when in such a state. Such signs become noticeable when, and are evidence that, cerebral damage has occurred.

Other signs are tenderness of the muscles and nerve trunks, with defects of sensation, referable to peripheral neuritis, and enlargement and tenderness of the liver which later gives way to shrinkage and induration.

Course and Prognosis
Although some resolute souls can wean themselves from spirits and can stage a dramatic recovery from the habit, the usual course of the untreated alcoholic is that of a pebble on a glacier, slow moving, but ever downwards.

Treatment
There is no treatment that will enable the established alcoholic addict to become a controlled drinker, although every alcoholic patient coming for treatment hopes for this result. The first essential is, therefore, to get the patient to accept that alcohol must be forsworn entirely and for ever. Patients will often reply that this makes the future look 'bleak'. The answer is that it is the only measure that will not make the future blank."

APPENDIX 3

DELIRIUM TREMENS

"Delirium Tremens is an acute brain syndrome due to alcohol intoxication, characterised by an acute hallucinatory delirium, and a coarse, generalised tremor which involves particularly the fingers, the face, and tongue.

Delirium may appear at any time in the chronic alcoholic, but it is usually precipitated by intercurrent infection, injury, or a prolonged debauch, or it may appear as an 'abstinence delirium' in the malignant, addictive alcoholic.

The syndrome begins suddenly with fever, rapid pulse, leukocytosis, profuse perspiration, headache, anorexia, nausea, weakness, and dehydration. Along with the tremor there are seen ataxia, hyperreflexia, and all these appear to be due to an encephalosis involving mainly the frontoponto-cerebellar pathways. Increased cerebro-spinal fluid pressure and increased globulin in the cerebro-spinal fluid are usual, and in about fifty per cent of cases, a mild transitory albuminuria is seen. Epileptiform convulsions may also occur; these 'rum fits', as they are sometimes called, are probably due to pyridoxine vitamin B6 deficiency.

The delirium itself begins within a few days after onset of the disorder. Persecutory delusions are common and are usually in reference to a gang of the same sex or some obvious castration fear. These delusions may lead to suicide or homicide; illusions are frequent and are easily suggested. Visual hallucinations are the most common of the hallucinatory elements, and these are typically of animals, such as snakes or rats, which symbolize mainly sexual fears (pink elephants, incidentally, are most uncommon). Haptic hallucinations, of animals crawling over the skin, are also seen, but many of these are probably illusions based on parathesiae. Auditory hallucinations, when they occur, are usually of a derogatory and/or homosexual nature.

In the midst of the delirium, disorientation is marked; there is loss of attention and memory impairment, most marked for recent memory. There is an incontinence of emotions: panic, anxiety, and terror most commonly, although some few show euphoria or indifference to their hallucinations and illusions. Mis-identification is common, and patients are highly suggestible and can easily be made to confabulate.

The delirium usually lasts three to six days; the patient usually has an amnesia for the delirium and frequently returns to his pattern of heavy drinking and thus there is often an early repetition of the syndrome. Auditory hallucinations usually indicate that the course will be prolonged. In uncomplicated cases, death is rare (3-4 per cent). If there is not full recovery, there is usually progression into a Korsakov syndrome (in about fifteen per cent of the cases).

The pathological picture consists of nuclear destruction of the nerve cells, with all degrees of granular degeneration and disintegration of the nuclei. In most patients, the cortex is mainly affected, but in those tending clinically to progress to a Korsakov psychosis, the brain stem is affected to a greater degree."
(Quoted from *The Psychiatric Dictionary*, by Leland E. Hinsie, M.D. and Robert J. Campbell, M.D.; published by Oxford Univ. Press.)

APPENDIX 4

'One more little drink won't do any harm!'

British television recently reported on attempts to rehabilitate chronic alcoholics.

The camera visited Glasgow, where buildings provided by charity keep several hundred alcoholics warm during inclement seasons. Three blocks from the city's most expensive hotel, busy volunteers welcomed inebriated fellows after closing time.

Spaces for the night appeared on tables, benches and the mattress-covered floor. (The facilities could not provide a shower for all; one hoped they slept with their shoes on.)

The viewer came within two feet of bodies laden with ethanol. Garbled songs and gut-level guffaws floated over swollen, violet tongues; leering grimaces and yellow-glazed, red-veined eye sockets described creatures found in C.W. Leadbeater's lowest plane of the astral world. C.W. Leadbeater was a late nineteenth-century clairvoyant who wrote many books describing the inner world and its inhabitants.

Two types of drinkers...

There are two types of alcoholics: the addict and the excuse-seeker. The first acquires his dependence through frequent over-indulgence. The habit creates a craving by the physical body for ethanol's depressing effects. The second person drinks to excuse himself from responsibility. He uses alcohol as an anaesthetic, 'to forget people and what you've done to them' as one (temporarily) sober fellow explained. His attitude of guilt lies on a psychological level: *Memory, Time's widow, is back, fretful of results* (See p.71, *The Spiritual Diary*, by D. Baker), and he attempts to drown her.

Let us mention that one of every three alcoholics is female.

Rest spots deal with immediate problems of the alcoholic. Shoes remain on feet for weeks; sores arise, become infected and require medication. Circulation of the blood slows, increasing the chances of gangrene and frostbite. Insecurity grows into a lack of will. The alcoholic seeks sympathy: *'I know I shouldn't, but I keep going back'.*

Experienced workers, often ex-alcoholics, base their choices for further treatment upon the individual's self-image. He will hardly cooperate with the discipline-to-come if he does not hold a dream to escape the bottle's grip.

The Journey of Rehabilitation

First, there comes the 'dry-up' at the hospital. A patient may choose to take a drug which causes stomach unrest if alcohol is swallowed. Through this unpleasant procedure, the sight of an alcoholic beverage will induce revulsion. Another method depends upon a healthy diet to distract the body. The stimuli of food will teach again the lesson of variety to a stomach that craves ethanol alone.

Next, the patient enters a mental discipline. He must free himself from psychological dependence. During this rehabilitation, a patient finds solace in a group. The members base their acquaintances on a common problem. They admit their weaknesses and identify their positive qualities of character; they aid each other in forming happier pictures of each other. The group develops concern for each member's success in sticking with the simple cure: *abstinence.*

The 'ethanolic' meets the final test when he returns to the community which fostered his indulgence. "Coming to the pub, Joe?"

The reply may cite 'a fear of beginning again' as a reason to stay away from the social centre. Or, as one fellow who took seven years to return to society says, "Yes, but only for a pint of cider."

'One more little drink' **will** harm some people.

APPENDIX 5

THE HIDDEN PATHOLOGY OF ALCOHOLISM

Cancer of the Throat and Mouth
The flow of energies into the brow region, thus enducing delirium tremens, indicates also that the same sort of energies flowing from the body into the head are reaching tissues en route or terminally via the Head Chakra and the centres in the throat.

Although much of the stimulation of tissues producing cancer of the oesophagus, larynx and the mouth come directly from the alcohol consumed, the etheric energies reinforce this action via the Throat Chakra and the Alta Major centre.

Stroke
The occurence of intracranial haemorrhage leading to loss of consciousness (stroke) and partial paralysis is related sometimes to drinking, especially binge drinking. However this relationship is procured, it is worth noting that in meditation, which is another way of increasing the flow of blood to the head and brain, the passage of etheric and pranic energies is also greatly increased to those regions. Meditation is not a

cure-all for the ills of mankind. It should never be practised by anyone who is ill and certainly not by anyone who has been drinking.

Cause Unknown

The comments above apply particularly to young people. Whether the stroke is caused by bleeding from blood vessels in the brain or through a thrombosis (blood clot), the relationship exists. Haemorrhagic stroke increases with greater consumption of alcohol quite independently of any other factors like high blood pressure or cigarette smoking. How alcohol produces this increased liability to stroke is *unknown.*

It must be repeated here that persistent drinking not only affects the brow region through over-stimulation of its chakra, but also the Head Chakra and nadis which interpenetrate the brain tissue and the blood vessels which supply it.

Heart Disease

The evidence of many studies shows that the incidence of heart disease is raised significantly in alcoholics. Again, we must seek out a hidden cause of this phenomenon in the etheric infra-structure of man. Over-stimulation of the Brow Chakra causes abnormal activity of the pituitary gland, which, amongst its many hormonal structures secretes an undiscovered factor which affects the uptake of nitrogen in the walls of arteries The following is quoted from another of the author's works, *Esoteric Healing, Part I*:

"The English Master, Robert Browning, taught me that a hormone from the anterior

pituitary gland, as yet undiscovered, is released with protein deprivation and this acts on the walls of the arteries in such a way that they begin to fix or take up nitrogen from the blood. There is a vast amount of nitrogen in solution conitnuously in the blood through its exposure to air in the lungs. The amounts of nitrogen taken up by the endothelial cells of arteries are minute but will one day, with even greater improvements in chemical analysis and methodology, be measureable.

Not all the arteries are thus affected. Those in the region of the Heart Chakra are most sensitive, and those that supply the brain are the next most receptive to the nitrogen. In this way, nature tries to compensate for deprivation of protein from the diet.

It would be nice to leave the matter there, but there are factors of even greater implication involved—else the subject would not have been released to me, as a medical doctor, by the English ashram in the first place.

Where there is excessive protein in the diet, and insufficient capacity of the individual to express himself fully (physically, emotionally and mentally) in conditions which we might group loosely under the expression of 'stress', there will occur overstimulation of the Ajna, or Brow Chakra with resultant excessive release of the hormonal factor indicated above, and the consequence is the uptake of nitrogenous mat-

erials of dietary and atmospheric origin to such an extent in the walls of the arteries, especially those in the Heart Chakra region (including the coronaries) that these deposits along with calcium and fatty mterials like cholesterol, would cause or accelerate deterioration of the artery walls and contribute to arterio-sclerosis and all of its death-dealing concomitants.

This does not mean that the reader should foolishly rush into protein deprivation. Far from it. Common sense in all such matters should prevail. Use all gently, as Shakespeare would say. Have periodic checkups with your medical practitioner if you undertake any sort of vegetarianism. Accompany all physical disciplines with meditation. Do not undertake any disciplines at all along these lines, if you are ill, mentally or physically. Get yourself well first, and then you are eligible for a serious treading of the Path."

The degeneration of blood vessels to the brain and to heart muscles causes more deaths than any other known factor. Esoteric evidence stems from a knowledge of the existence of the chakras.

The Heart Chakra lies very close to the coronary arteries which are so susceptible to degenerative processes. Malfunction, either through over-stimulation or under-activity, of the Heart Chakra is a killer. The added aggravation of alcoholic abuse is deadly where a constitution is already weakened by other factors like malnutrition, hypertension, smoking etc. (See diagram.)

When the author was at medical school he was taught that a little drinking did no harm... say, a glass of wine with a meal. Some even said that statistics show that those who indulge themselves thus tended to do better than those who did not drink at all.

The following report from the Encyclopaedia Britannica (Medical and Health) may clear up some of the confusion.

> *In a study of stroke incidence among nearly 8,000 men who were followed over a 12-year period in the Honolulu Heart Program, researchers found that light drinkers had more than double the risk of hemorrhagic stroke than non-drinkers. Among heavy drinkers the risk was nearly triple. The relationship between excessive alcohol consumption and increased risk of stroke is less certain than the link that has been established for such chronic diseases as cirrhosis of the liver, hypertension, and nervous system disorders.*

APPENDIX 6

SOME SPIRITUAL SIGNIFICANCES OF ALCOHOLISM

Earlier in this book were quoted those most significant words of Carl Jung...*"the craving for alcohol is the equivalent, on a low level, of the spiritual thirst of our being for wholeness, expressed in medieval language: the union with God."*

Those who are enslaved by alcohol will always tell you that the upward climb out of that condition is the hardest one to scale in all human suffering.

The author begs to differ. That dreadful struggle upwards, out of enmeshment into clarity and sobriety, is but a learning ground for what comes inexorably thereafter.

Many lives may pass before the ultimate, merciless struggle of which I speak. No person escapes. At least one life is given to alcoholism. Usually there is a series of such lives followed by more lives free from spiritual thirst.

The ultimate is to integrate a personality of

no mean quality and then to surrender it to the very spiritual essence that makes so many thirst. This marks the end of human existence, a termination that follows hundreds of lives in human earthly forms. Thereafter, as a spiritual being, there are other goals to reach for.

The spiritual struggle towards wholeness and freedom from rebirth passes through the stages of discipleship, initiation and finally reaches the 'burning ground' whereon the final nature is purged of imperfection. No-one can escape the process though many will put the finale off for many lives.

An escape into alcoholism will only quench the thirst for spirit for a comparatively short time, perhaps for just three or four lives. He who fights his way back to abstinence will be more ready for the greater struggle towards spiritual light.

Only the personality which is completely integrated, in which all three bodies, the physical, emotional, and mental, are fully developed and completely under the control of the ego, is able to endure, nay, even survive the application of the planetary rod of initiation to the head centres clustered about the third ventricle of the brain, the core of the magnetic aura.

Only he who has been malleable, tempered, and tested in the hall of experience is ready for the hall of initiation. Anyone less eligible would not get past even the Dweller on the Threshold, let alone survive the flash of planetary fire on the Burning Ground.

If you have never known the sickening thrill of a straight flush, if you have never paused, guilty, 'in the rank sweat of an ensemened bed', or clapped your hands to ears that would shut out the screams of scorching tank-entombed men, or, true blue, have never quelled the nausea of protesting organs with gulps of C_2OH_5, or, friendless, in the great alone, have never heard the winds speak, or the earth move, or hounded by some unknown force, have not plunged deep in every glittering pool and have not emerged from all of these crying ever, 'Not this! Not this!' —then these words are not for you.

The Burning Ground is not for you, not yet, not until every call of the flesh is answered, not until every material mesh has clung to you. But, when richest in experience, experience beyond your wildest dreams, and when poorest in attachment to them, then comes the Burning Ground.

By the same author:

THE JEWEL IN THE LOTUS
BEYOND THE INTELLECT
MEDITATION, The Theory & Practice
ESOTERIC ANATOMY, Vols. I & II
ESOTERIC ASTROLOGY, Vols. I—X
ESOTERIC PSYCHOLOGY, The Seven Rays
HANDBOOK OF THE SEVEN RAYS
THE PSYCHOLOGY OF DISCIPLESHIP
BACH FLOWER REMEDY REPERTOIRES
ESOTERIC HEALING, Vols. I—III
THE TECHNIQUES OF ASTRAL PROJECTION
THE PHENOMENA OF MATERIALISATION
PARACELSUS, His Methods of Healing
ANTHROPOGENY
THE SPIRITUAL DIARY
THE DIARY OF AN ALCHEMIST
LIFE AFTER DEATH
REINCARNATION
STRESS DISORDERS
ALCOHOLISM
THE HUMAN AURA
THE EGOIC LOTUS
KARMIC LAWS
THE THIRD EYE
THE OPENING OF THE THIRD EYE
THE POWERS LATENT IN MAN
SUPERCONSCIOUSNESS THROUGH MEDITATION
and many more

STRESS DISORDERS

The traditional orthodox attitude with regard to the growing problem of stress has invariably been to find ways of relieving that stress by whatever means possible. Usually this has been through excessive smoking and drinking which, in the end, has served only to aggravate the problem. For Man on the Path however, the factor of stress is not something which must be eliminated at all costs, but, on the contrary is something which he must learn to thrive on, for without it he would be incapable of evolving spiritually. The problem arises when he is confronted with excessive amounts of stress which result in *dis*-tress.

Here, for the first time, a medical practitioner deals with the subject of stress from an esoteric viewpoint. He discusses how these stress disorders may arise and gives us practical advice as well as exercises on how to treat them.

LIFE AFTER DEATH

The subject of death and the possibility of an afterlife has been the constant source of Man's greatest fear as well as fascination. Right from his earliest days he has asked himself these puzzling questions:

> Is death painful?
> Do we survive the grave?
> What do we survive in?
> Where do we go after death?

In those early days these questions were answered, usually inadequately, by the contemporary religion. It is only now, free from the restraints of religious dogma, that we may ask these questions afresh.

In this book, Dr. Douglas Baker, not only a qualified medical practitioner, but also an occulist of more than 40 years' experience, answers these as well as many other questions related to life after death. His conclusions are based on actual case-histories and, more important, on his own personal exploration of the inner worlds where he has been a witness to many of the events described herein.

THE POWERS LATENT IN MAN

The powers discussed by Dr. Baker are exercised by a minority of psychically gifted people, but they are latent in all of us. These powers include hypnosis, telepathy, psychokinesis, and healing. Dr. Baker presents scientific and 'mystical' evidence for the existence of these mysterious but natural forces, and documents their operation in contemporary society. Amongst the amazing subjects covered in this book are: super-gifted children; auric manipulation for intellectual power, continued youthfulness, and mental brilliance; the regeneration of amputated limbs with negative electric current and the reasons behind heart transplantation failure. Dr. Baker's exciting proposition in this book is that the esoteric and occult truths of the ages are being verified by science.

THE OCCULT SIGNIFICANCE OF UFO'S

No doubt one of the greatest mysteries to emerge from the latter half of the twentieth century has been the subject of UFO's. The questions on everyone's lips at the moment are: *Do flying saucers really exist?* and *Has our Earth at any time been visited by extra-terrestrials?*

In this book, Dr. Douglas Baker, an investigator into the phenomena of UFO's for more than 25 years, states conclusively that yes, our Earth has indeed been visited by extra-terrestrials from as far back us 18 million years ago, with the advent of the 'Lords of the Flame'. He goes on to say that although many of the sightings can be explained away by science as simple natural occurences, there remain the few isolated incidents which defy all present scientific means of interpretation. Dr. Baker's conclusions are startling.